Wine by Style

Wine by Style

A practical guide to choosing wine by flavour, body, and colour

Fiona Beckett

Mitchell Beazley

Wine by Style
by Fiona Beckett

First published in Great Britain in 1998 by Mitchell Beazley, an imprint of Octopus Publishing
Group Ltd, 2–4 Heron Quays, London E14 4JP

Revised edition 2006

ISBN 1 84533 200 8

A CIP record of this book is available from the British Library

Set in Foundry
Printed and bound in China by Toppan Printing Company Limited

Commissioning Editor: Sue Jamieson, Hilary Lumsden
Executive Art Editor: Fiona Knowles, Yasia Williams-Leedham
Editor: Lucy Bridgers, Juanne Branquinho
Design: Geoff Fennell,
Cover Design: Gaelle Lochner
Specially commissioned photography: Steven Morris
Production: Rachel Lynch, Ann Childers, Gary Hayes
Picture Research: Anna Kobryn, Juanne Branquinho
Index: Angie Hipkin

CONTENTS

INTRODUCTION

When you first start drinking and buying wine, it can be a bewildering experience – a world that everybody seems to know more about than you. There are so many wines, so many confusing and unfamiliar names, that it seems impossible to get to grips with them all.

Gradually, as you try different wines, you will find a few that you really enjoy. In sheer relief you may be tempted to buy them again and again. Then it's all too easy to get stuck in a rut, often paying more than you need for a wine that has ceased to be good value.

Wine by Style is all about giving you the confidence to take your acquaintance with wine a step further by helping you to identify the styles of wine you enjoy. It takes a radically different approach to many wine books. Instead of looking in-depth at the various wine producing regions of the world (an exercise you may well want to pursue at some point, but which can be daunting when you're starting out), I've concentrated on certain easily recognizable wine styles with which you're probably already familiar. Once you find a wine you enjoy, all you have to do is check out which other wines are made in the same style.

There's an important point to underline at this stage. People sometimes worry that if they prefer, say, a medium dry white to a red Bordeaux, there is something to be apologetic about. But there isn't a "right" and "wrong" style of wine. You only have to consider how tastes differ with respect to food: some people are sweet-toothed, some are not; some love to eat salads, others avoid them; people's tolerance of spicy food varies hugely. It would be surprising (and very dull) if we all liked the same wines.

Your tastes in wine may also change. When you start drinking it you may well be more attracted to a fresh, fruity white wine than a full-bodied red. Later you may prefer wines with a stronger, more intense flavour. This is normal. If you draw a parallel with coffee, people rarely start with a double espresso; they choose a latte or capuccino and only gradually move on to drinking their coffee black.

It is unlikely, therefore, that just one style of wine will suit you. Your tastes may change at different stages in your life. When you first start drinking wine in your twenties or thirties, you may be attracted by simple fruit flavours. Twenty years on, when you've had a chance to taste a much wider range of wines, you may look for wines of greater maturity, subtlety, and complexity. You can get bored with a style of wine, such as heavily oaked Chardonnay, and start to look for something new. And, of course, wines themselves change. Since the first edition of this book was published different white wines like Albariño, Grüner Veltliner, and Viognier have come to the forefront, reds have become progressivley more full-bodied, and rosés have become far, far more fashionable, offering a much wider range of choice than was the case even a few years ago.

Your choice of wine may also change with your mood or the time of year. The fresh, crisp rosé you enjoyed so much on holiday is not necessarily going to be as appealing in the middle of the winter when there's frost outside. Similarly, a big gutsy red will just seem too heavy when the weather's warm and summery. And if you want to celebrate, you're far more likely to crack open a bottle of Champagne or sparkling wine to mark the occasion than a dry white wine.

The style of wine you pick also depends on the type of food you're eating – and who you're eating it with. As you can see from the Wine and Food section at the back of the book (pages 104–9), certain styles of wine suit certain foods. A light, crisp white wine, for example, would be overwhelmed by a rich, intensely flavoured beef dish. Even if light white wine is normally the style you prefer, you would probably be looking for a fruity red to match the beef.

Equally, you may want to take into account the likely preferences of your guests. More individual wines, such as aromatic whites, aged red wines and rarities, are not to everyone's taste. If you have guests whose taste in wine you're uncertain about, you would be better searching in the smooth, medium-bodied white and red sections.

It may also surprise you to learn that how you treat a bottle of wine (how long you keep it for and the temperature at which you serve it, for instance) can affect its style, so I have included a section on how to store and serve wine and how to recognise wine faults.

All this is not to replace one daunting set of rules with another, but is more an invitation to roam freely through the book and not to rule out certain styles of wine. Wine drinking should be a pleasure, not a trial. I hope this book brings that experience one step nearer for you.

Fiona Beckett, July 2005

WHAT INFLUENCES STYLE AND FLAVOUR?

At one time most winemakers didn't really make a conscious decision about what style of wine to produce. If they were working within the framework of rules that applied to the vineyards in their area – as most producers did in countries such as France and Italy – there was little choice about the varieties they could plant, when to harvest or how many grapes the vines produced. Then, even more than now, winemakers were at the mercy of the weather. If the vineyards were hit by frost, little could be done about it. If it was sweltering hot when the time came to make the wine, it was hard to keep the temperature in the winery under control.

Now the situation is totally different. In many parts of the world, particularly in the newer winemaking countries of Australia, Chile, South Africa, and New Zealand, that rigid framework of rules does not exist. Within the constraints of their resources, equipment, and manpower, winemakers can do as they like. The huge hi-tech wineries of today can fashion more or less any kind of wine the market wants.

The most influential people are no longer the bureaucrats who administer the rules, but the buyers for large supermarket chains. It's debatable how healthy this is. There has been justifiable concern about the extent to which the individuality of different wine-producing regions has been lost and about how wines are tasting the same whichever part of the world they come from. Yet it can't be denied that the general standard of wine is higher than it has ever been.

For all the technical progress that has occurred, the fact remains that wine is an agricultural product and that the most important influences on its style are the type of grape that it is made from and the climate in which these grapes are grown. These and other influences are explored over the next few pages.

Grape varieties

The importance of the grape or grapes that a wine is made from is recognized by the fact that the most familiar wines to the majority of wine drinkers are varietals – wines named after grape varieties such as Chardonnay and Cabernet Sauvignon. The most popular varieties are called "noble" grapes because they are used to make some of the world's greatest wines. Increasing attention, however, is being focused on lesser-known grapes which offer new and different flavours. Over the next few years you can expect to see more of less familiar varieties such as Bonarda, Carmenère, Garganega, and Nero d'Avola.

Climate and soil

The French concept of terroir (the unique combination of climate, soil, and situation) is now recognized throughout the world as increasingly important to the production of quality wines. New World winemakers may have once believed that they could achieve anything in the winery, but they have come to recognize the importance of picking sites best suited to the grape variety they want to plant.

Winemaking techniques

The advances in winemaking techniques, particularly temperature control and the use of cultured yeasts, have revolutionized the production of cheaper wines. It is now possible to produce fresh, clean, characterful wines out of what even ten years ago would have been unpromising raw materials. The palate of flavours available to the modern winemaker is more sophisticated than it has ever been.

Oak

Not all wines, of course, are oaked, but the influence of different kinds of barrels can be dramatic. Oak can be either an obvious influence or a subtle one, depending on the effect the winemaker is striving for. In general, the presence of oak will result in a more full-bodied style of wine, though the extent of that depends on the age of the wine.

How these variables interact in a finished wine is a complex and fascinating process. The next few pages explore them further.

GRAPE VARIETIES

It is the grape variety or blend of varieties that gives wine its defining character. That may seem obvious – you can hardly make a red wine out of white grapes (although winemakers do occasionally make white out of red) – but the influence of grape varieties amounts to more than that. Regardless of climate or modern techniques, if you harvest a crop of Chardonnay, for example, you know you're not going to end up with a wine that smells of grass or gooseberries.

Of course this is more true of some grapes than of others. You're unlikely to taste a dry Italian white and say "Aha, Trebbiano!". But the world's most expensive, high-quality grapes such as Chardonnay and Cabernet Sauvignon have powerful personalities that make wines made from them easily identifiable.

Varietal labelling

It was this ease of recognition that led the Californians (never a slouch at marketing) during the 1970s to name and label their wines after the grape variety they were made from. This move has probably had more impact on the wine-drinking world than anything else in recent years. Varietals – the name given to wines made from a single grape variety – have given wine drinkers great confidence. Not only is it easier to predict what a wine will taste like, but we can also remember and pronounce its name without making fools of ourselves. The French are even putting the name of the grape on such traditional wines as burgundy.

This emphasis on grape varieties has also had an effect on quality. The traditional way of making wine – still practised in Bordeaux and many other parts of Europe – used to be to blend several grape varieties together. If you had problems with the weather when you were harvesting one grape, you could always increase the percentage of another. Where winemakers don't have that option to fall back on, they have to ensure that the basic quality of their grapes is as high as possible and that they're handled as carefully as possible in the winery.

So why then does a wine from the same grape variety sometimes taste so different? There are many factors at play and the most important is climate. Generally, vines grown in hot, sunny climates will have richer, riper fruit flavours than vines grown in cool, unpredictable ones. This is particularly evident in the northern hemisphere, where weather conditions at harvest time can vary significantly from one year to another. A good vintage will result in a more full-bodied style; a poor vintage in a lighter, tarter one.

Other factors that play a part are the clones (the specific strain of a grape variety) that are planted, how old the vines are (older vines tend to make more expressive wines than younger ones) and how prolifically they're allowed to grow. If you allow vines to produce as many grapes as they can, you'll end up with a lighter, more dilute wine than if you restrict the yield or select only the best bunches.

Grapes, soils, and ageing

Some grapes are ideally suited to certain sites – an affinity that the French enshrine in their strict *appellation contrôlée* system. Pinot Noir, for example, is perfectly suited to the relatively cool climate and limestone soils of Burgundy. (In fact, a grape like Cabernet Franc would probably grow happily there too, but the French believe, with some justification, that it blurs the distinctiveness of wines produced in different regions to allow winemakers to plant any grape they want.)

The character of a grape can also be modified or enhanced in the winery, most notably by the presence or absence of oak and whether or not the grape is blended with other varieties. A Chardonnay that is made in a stainless-steel tank and released within a few months of harvesting will be lighter and crisper than one aged in a barrel for months. It will also be less obviously like Chardonnay if it is blended with another strongly flavoured grape such as Sémillon or Sauvignon Blanc, or even with a small proportion of an aromatic grape such as Viognier. (In many wine producing regions producers can include up to twenty per cent of other grapes in a blend without having to state it on the label.)

The final important factor that can affect the way a grape tastes is age. Most wines nowadays are sold within months of being bottled and consumed within days of being bought. But if you buy an older wine or keep it for a long time before you drink it, you will notice a marked change from the lively fruity character it had when it was young, a change you may or may not welcome.

The chances are that if you like one wine made from a specific grape variety, you'll like others made from the same variety, but that won't always be the case. Young, unoaked Tempranillo is as different from mature Rioja as Australian Chardonnay is from Chablis. Although most people have embraced the fruity flavours of New World wines, others find them far too sweet and hanker for drier, more traditional versions.

The key is to know more about the styles of wine that are made with different grapes. Here are the ones you're most likely to come across.

Above *These cool European vineyards (Médoc), even when planted with the same grape variety as hot New World vineyards such as in California (**far left**), will produce wines with quite different flavours. The cooler the climate, the leaner the flavours. Conversely, in hotter climates the wines have distinctly more tropical fruit flavours.*

WHITE GRAPES

Chardonnay

This grape variety is so popular these days that it is almost like a brand name. Most people associate it with the big fruity flavours of Australia and California without realising that it is the same grape that produces such well-known white burgundies as Chablis and that it is an important component of Champagne.

Why is Chardonnay so popular? Because it pleases just about everyone. The winemaker appreciates the fact that the grape is easy to grow and able to adapt itself to whatever he or she wants to do with it. The wine-drinker enjoys the wide range of taste sensations it offers, from crisp, fresh, and citrussy to powerfully full-bodied and oaky. The common denominator of all Chardonnay wines is that they tend to be smooth and creamy as opposed to crisply acidic like a Riesling or Sauvignon Blanc.

The major differences in style reflect the climate in which the grapes are grown. Chardonnay made from grapes grown in a cool region such as Chablis and the rest of Burgundy is leaner, drier, and more neutral in flavour than Chardonnay made from grapes grown in warmer regions such as South Australia, Hawkes Bay in New Zealand, South Africa, and California, which have much riper, more tropical fruit flavours. In cooler regions of the New World such as the Marlborough region of New Zealand that difference may be less obvious.

The wine will also be markedly different depending on whether or not it is oaked. Unoaked Chardonnay has crisp, clean fruit flavours (drier in Burgundy, riper in the southern hemisphere), while oaked Chardonnay ranges from the elegant creamy, nutty wines of Burgundy and California, to the more toasty oaky flavours of the less expensive Chardonnays of Argentina and South Africa.

Chardonnay's character may also be diluted when it is blended with another grape such as Semillon, Sauvignon Blanc, or Viognier.

Sauvignon Blanc

An extraordinary range of styles are embraced by this variety, though most people associate it with the exuberant gooseberry flavour that is typical of New Zealand and to a lesser extent Loire Sauvignons. Like Chardonnay, it reveals different personalities depending on where it is planted, but its most appealing character and crisp acidity really only develops in cooler growing areas.

Sauvignon Blanc also responds less well than Chardonnay to oak, which tends to mask rather than enhance its natural crisp acidity. In top Sauvignons oak can give the wine added richness and longevity. In younger wines such as California's Fumé Blanc style, it creates a different, much softer style of wine that won't necessarily appeal if you are a Sauvignon aficionado. For most producers there is little point in oaking because inexpensive Sauvignon is best consumed while young.

The heartland of Sauvignon production is the Loire Valley, which produces a distinctively crisp, minerally, flinty style most commonly encountered in Sancerre and Pouilly-Fumé though inexpensive Sauvignon de Touraine offers this style at a very reasonable price. In Bordeaux the grape achieves greatness combined with Sémillon, though it also makes pleasant, fresh, citrussy wines on its own. Elsewhere in Europe the best bargains are found in Hungary and northern Italy.

In the southern hemisphere, New Zealand's Marlborough region has become the benchmark for New World Sauvignon, delivering a piercing intensity of fruit that has a unique character. Its pre-eminence is increasingly being challenged by Chile, South Africa, and the Adelaide Hills region of Southern Australia, all of which have producers who make some fine, elegant wines as well as a lot of simple, straightforward, citrussy Sauvignons that offer excellent value.

Riesling

Although it is capable of producing some of the world's finest and most individual wines, Riesling can be difficult to get used to. In its youth it can be sharply acidic and can take several years to develop those luscious oily, petrolly flavours that so please its devotees. But there is no other grape quite like it. Infinitely refreshing, elegant, and juicy, it's like biting into a perfectly ripe grape.

Germany is indisputably the home of great Riesling, though it varies from region to region from the thrillingly racy acidity of the Mosel to more opulent, rich, spicy flavours of the Pfalz and Rheingau. In levels of sweetness it varies from fresh, crisp, appley Kabinetts to sumptuously sweet Beerenauslesen and Trockenbeerenauslesen. Serious Rieslings are also produced in Alsace, where they tend to be richer and more alcoholic than the German examples, and in the Wachau, Kremstal, and Kampstal regions of Austria.

Riesling has also found a natural home in the New World in the cooler growing areas of South Australia (especially the Clare and Eden

Above *Sauvignon Blanc is a highly adaptable grape variety. Classic examples are from the upper reaches of the Loire Valley in France and are lean, crisp and grassy. More pungent, intensely flavoured examples come from New Zealand.*

Far left *Chardonnay is not simply the name of a wine. It is a grape variety producing wines that range from crisp, minerally wines from Chablis, Mâcon, and northern Italy, right through to the rich, tropical fruit-flavoured wines of California and Australia.*

Valleys), where it develops a richer, limier, and, for first time Riesling drinkers, a more attractively fruity character. The grape also does well in New Zealand, Canada, and New York State.

Semillon

This grape is less appreciated than it deserves to be because it is often blended. On its own it makes richly textured wines with wonderful flavours of caramelised pineapple and tropical fruits. That pineapple flavour still comes through when it is combined with other grapes (most commonly Sauvignon Blanc and Chardonnay), but Semillon rarely gets the credit.

In the Hunter Valley in New South Wales it produces almost Riesling-style wines that last for years. But it is the real star of white wine-making in Bordeaux where, with Sauvignon, it produces fine dry whites along with the famous sweet wine, Sauternes.

Important but lesser-known white grape varieties

Colombard A high yielding grape variety that in France serves the dual role of providing the base for Cognac and Armagnac and of producing crisp, uncomplicated, slightly floral white wines, most notably Vin de Pays des Côtes de Gascogne.

Colombard is also planted in the New World in California, South Africa, and Australia, where it develops a riper, more tropical fruit flavour and can be used as an inexpensive substitute for, or blended with, Chardonnay.

Chenin Blanc A popular workhorse of a grape in the New World, especially South Africa, Chenin Blanc is capable of producing far more interesting, rich dry wines in the Chardonnay style than one might assume from the cheaper examples on the market.

In the Loire Valley in France, it is almost a different grape altogether; used to make a range of dry, off-dry, and sweet wines with incredibly honeyed flavours that develop with age.

Gewürztraminer A love-it-or-loathe-it variety with a highly distinctive, pungent character, this grape's taste has been compared to lychees, rose petals, and Turkish delight. Its finest expression is in Alsace in France, where it is used to make remarkable, luscious, long-lived, semi-sweet and dessert wines. There is also increasing interest in

Gewürztraminer (or Gewürz, as it is known for short) in the New World. South Africa, Chile and New Zealand all offer attractively fruity examples.

Muscat Of all grape varieties, this one tastes the most truly grapey. Although you may come across it in dry wines labelled as "Dry Muscat" or in blends, its reputation is built on dessert wines. It presents itself in an extraordinary number of guises, from the soft, gently sparkling Moscato d'Asti, to the light, honeyed, refreshing Moscatel de Valencia, and the rich, sweet, fortified Muscats of southern France such as Muscat de Beaumes de Venise. Muscat is also grown in the Rutherglen region of Victoria in Australia, where it produces a richly toffeed liqueur wine.

Pinot Gris/Pinot Grigio The two names this grape goes by reflect two very different styles. Pinot Grigio, as it is known in Italy and California, produces a typically crisp, clean white wine that should be drunk as young as possible. Pinot Gris, which is a speciality of the Alsace region of France, is richer and more opulent, producing wines that range in style from dry and full-bodied to luxuriously sweet and that have an impressive capacity for ageing. There has also been a fair amount of New World interest in it, particularly in New Zealand and Oregon, as a stylish alternative to Chardonnay.

Roussanne Increasingly fashionable white wine grape, originally from the Rhône where it is used to make the rare but seriously impressive white Hermitage that can last for decades. Like Viognier (*see* below), it has opulent, peachy fruit, but is more restrained, producing elegant, dry wines that work well with all kinds of food. In the south of France, it is frequently blended with other varieties such as Marsanne and Viognier, but is attracting attention as a solo performer in California and elsewhere in the New World.

Viognier An increasingly popular variety especially in southern France – where it is now widely grown in the Languedoc – and in Australia and California, as well as in its original home of the Rhône. Notable for producing full-bodied, apricot-scented whites, it is also used in blends with varieties such as Marsanne and Roussanne, where a small amount can have a noticeable impact.

Above *Gewürztraminer, with its delicately pink grapes, is something you either love or hate. The wine it produces has distinctively exotic aromas and is often the perfect foil for Chinese and Southeast Asian cuisine.*

Far left *Riesling is a grape variety that produces some of the world's most exciting wines. Its refreshing acidity gives the wines great elegance. As they range from crisp and appley to lusciously sweet and honeyed, they partner a wide variety of food.*

RED GRAPES

Cabernet Sauvignon

This grape is to red wine what Chardonnay is to white – almost every winemaker wants to plant it and every wine-lover wants to drink it.

It is distinguished by small, thick-skinned grapes which give structure and body, making it suitable for long ageing. Seldom light-bodied, one Cabernet wine can be very different from another. Cabernet from the comparatively northern region of Bordeaux produces dry, elegant, occasionally austere wines. When it comes from the much hotter southern hemisphere, a vibrant blackcurrant character is more evident.

Even within Bordeaux there is a world of difference between the simple fruit of a young claret and the complex cedary elegance of a ten-year-old classed growth from a great vintage. Traditionally, Cabernet-dominated wines come from the so-called "Left Bank" of the Gironde, from famous Médoc villages such as St-Estèphe, St-Julien, Pauillac, and Margaux. Even though they are blended with a proportion of Merlot, they are characteristically leaner and less fruity than those from the Merlot dominated "Right Bank".

An altogether fruitier style is produced in the New World, particularly in the Coonawarra region of South Australia, where the wines acquire an intensely lush, minty character. Chile produces wines that have a particularly vivid fruit flavour, while South Africa's tend to be classically more European in character. The wine-growing region that models its Cabernets most closely on the classic French style is California, whose wines rival Bordeaux in both quality and price.

Merlot

Merlot has never really attracted the same enthusiastic fan-base as Cabernet despite the fact that it is used in famous Bordeaux wines such as Châteaux Pétrus and Le Pin. But it has benefited hugely from New World interest because its supple fruit makes it a more approachable starting point for the growing number of new red wine drinkers.

Merlot's character also doesn't vary as much as Cabernet. Even without oak it generally makes a soft fruity red, though more expensive versions will develop a particularly velvety texture or rich, lush chocolatey tones.

Unlike Cabernet Sauvignon, Merlot seldom suffers from being under ripe and drinks as enjoyably when it is young and fruity as it does with a year or two of bottle age.

In the New World the most exciting Merlots are to be found in Chile and up on the west coast of America in California and Washington State. South African Merlot can be robustly plummy, while in New Zealand the grape is being blended with their slightly lean Cabernet to very good effect.

Pinot Noir

They say you're either a Cabernet or a burgundy fan, but for Pinot Noir devotees there's simply no contest. Other grapes may come in and out of fashion, but there is no grape that matches it for sheer sensuality.

Fine Pinot Noir is an elusive goal. Good burgundy is as much about feel as flavour and not many areas can achieve that thrillingly fine, silky, texture of the greatest burgundies. On the other hand for most of the Pinots the majority of us can afford the new World provides much more consistently reliable drinking. A whole raft of Pinot Noirs are now available from countries and regions such as New Zealand, California, Oregon, Chile, South Africa, and Australia's Yarra Valley that offer enough scintillatingly ripe, raspberry fruit to make any Pinot Noir devotee happy.

Pinot Noir is also successfully grown in Austria (where it is known as Blauburgunder), Germany (where it is called Spätburgunder) and Switzerland.

Syrah/Shiraz

Many people don't realise that these are one and the same grape. It produces gutsy wines with a characteristic smoky, slightly tarry aroma, vivid red berry fruit, and a distinctive spicy, peppery finish.

Traditionally the finest examples have come from the northern Rhône, producing concentrated, yet elegant wines, such as Hermitage, Cornas, and Côte Rôtie. It is also widely planted in southern France, where it is often blended with other southern grapes such as Grenache and Mourvedre creating attractively rich, supple reds. There are also some excellent Spanish examples.

But the country that has done more than any other to put Shiraz (as they call it) on the map is Australia. Much sweeter and fruitier than French Syrah, it has the same impressive concentration. There is also Syrah in Argentina, some in California, and an increasing amount in South Africa (where they also call it Shiraz).

Above *Merlot has a softer, more approachable style than Cabernet Sauvignon and in the clay soils of St-Emilion and Pomerol, on Bordeaux's Right Bank, it produces two of the world's most expensive and illustrious wines – Châteaux Pétrus and Le Pin.*

Far left *Cabernet Sauvignon has small berries, thick skins, high levels of pips, and is ideally suited to extended oak ageing. Cabernet makes wines that, at their finest, can age for decades and the majority of these come from Bordeaux's Médoc district.*

Important but lesser-known red grape varieties

Cabernet Franc Cabernet Franc is the unsung hero of Bordeaux – a valuable component of many blends thanks to its ability to ripen earlier and tolerate cool weather better than Cabernet Sauvignon. Cabernet Franc is lighter, fruitier, and more acidic than the other Cabernet, although in parts of the New World such as California, South Africa, New York, and Washington State Cabernet Franc is capable of producing wines of great power and personality.

Cabernet Franc is also widely found in southwest France, Eastern Europe, and the Friuli region of Italy. But the area where it really shines is in the central part of the Loire Valley, where it produces charmingly elegant, fruity reds such as Bourgueil, Chinon, and Saumur-Champigny.

Gamay Most people have heard of Beaujolais, but few realise that Gamay is the grape from which the wine is made. It has a distinctive character – light, juicy, and fruity with (when it is made in a *nouveau* style) an inimitable bubble-gum-and-banana flavour and aroma. It is also found in the Loire, where it is used to make Beaujolais-style reds.

Grenache/Garnacha The world's most widely planted red wine grape, this is a silent partner in many of the Rhône's best known reds (from Côtes du Rhône to Châteauneuf-du-Pape), and in the wines of the Languedoc-Roussillon and Spain. Generously prolific, Grenache has traditionally been used for rather light, dilute strawberry flavoured reds, but renewed interest in it, and particularly in the wines that can be produced from older vines, has resulted in lusher, more full-bodied examples. Some fine New World Grenache wines are emerging from Australia and California where, along with other Rhône varieties, Grenache has been enthusiastically embraced.

Mourvèdre A richly perfumed yet powerful grape variety that features in many southern French reds, especially in Provence where it is the dominant variety in Bandol. It is also widely planted in southern Spain where it is called Monastrell and produces powerful, full-bodied gamey reds such as Jumilla. In Australia it is called Mataro and is often blended with Shiraz.

Nebbiolo This grape variety is the backbone of two of north west Italy's greatest reds, Barolo and Barbaresco. A deeply flavoured, dense, late-ripening variety, it has unyielding tannins that can take several years of wood maturation to smooth out, but the results can be magnificent. As with other grape varieties, winemakers are now using Nebbiolo to make more vibrant, fruitier wines but which still pack a considerable punch. There's also interest in this grape in Australia and California.

Pinotage A cross between Pinot Noir and Cinsault (or Hermitage, as it used to be called), Pinotage is unique to South Africa. Its character depends critically on how it's made. If the vines are allowed to crop prolifically it produces simple, gluggable, sweetish reds. If yields are kept low and the grapes come from old vines, it can produce deliciously deep, richly concentrated full-bodied wines.

Sangiovese Widely used in Italy for the production of Chianti and many other Italian reds, Sangiovese most commonly results in light, fruity, supple wines with relatively high levels of acidity. In some denominations such as Brunello di Montalcino, and as a component of so-called Super-Tuscans, it makes very serious wine indeed. It has also become increasingly popular in Argentina and California.

Tempranillo Spain's most highly regarded grape goes by a confusing variety of names: Tempranillo in Rioja (of which it is a major component), Tinto Fino in Ribera del Duero, and Cencibel in Valdepeñas. Young, unoaked Tempranillo is vividly fruity, but that character has often been subdued by extended oak contact, particularly in wines labelled "Reserva" or "Gran Reserva" which have spent several years in cask and bottle before they are released. The resulting wines have a distinctive soft strawberry fruit taste. Tempranillo is also increasingly popular in Argentina and is being grown on an experimental basis elsewhere, most notably in Australia and California.

Zinfandel Widely planted in California where it makes an extraordinary range of wines, from sweet blush coloured "white" Zinfandel to richly alcoholic "killer Zins" of fourteen degrees or more. As with most reds price is a reliable indicator of style, the more expensive bottles being the most full-bodied and intense.' In Southern Italy it goes under the name Primitivo. There have also been some successful examples from South Africa.

Above *Syrah (Shiraz) produces some of the world's most powerful wines. The benchmark examples come from the northern Rhône in France and from the Barossa and Hunter Valleys in Australia. They have the common characteristic of being dark coloured and tannic with intense fruit and peppery spice.*

Far left *Pinot Noir, in contrast, produces some of the most delicate and subtle red wines. It is notoriously difficult to handle, being susceptible to mould, but can produce exquisitely ethereal, sensuous wines and consequently has legions of loyal followers.*

CLIMATE, SOIL, AND VINES

If there's one thing Old and New World winemakers agree about it is the need for top quality grapes. With them the least talented winemaker can make decent wine. Without them even the best will struggle.

But how do you produce them? In Europe, especially France, traditionally, the best way to ensure quality is to find a vineyard with the ideal soil, position, and climate for the grapes you want to grow – what the the French call terroir. This is enshrined in the closely monitored set of rules and regulations of the *appellation contrôlée* system which determines which grape varieties can be used, how densely they can be planted, and how many grapes (how great a yield) they can produce.

For newer wine-producing countries, the emphasis up to now has been more on the management of the vineyard – how to prune and train the vines to best ripen the fruit. There are no hang-ups about irrigation or about machine pruning or harvesting – everything is done to maximise the efficiency of the vines.

As with other aspects of winemaking, the divisions between the two approaches are less clear cut than they once were. French winemakers now pay more attention to training and pruning. Australian wine-producers are more aware of the advantages of planting the right grapes on the right site. More important than either tradition these days is the type of wine being made – whether it is an inexpensive wine for immediate consumption or a fine wine that will command a high price and therefore justifies extra attention in the vineyard and site selection.

But even the most meticulous planning and control cannot wholly determine how a wine turns out. Grapes are a natural harvest like any other and in the end they depend on something that is fundamentally unpredictable – the weather.

The importance of climate

Vines are hardy plants but they will not grow just anywhere. Too cold and the grapes won't ripen. Too hot and they won't develop the fresh fruity flavours you're looking for. To cultivate vines successfully you need a sufficiently cold winter so that the plants can close down and regain their vigour, which is why people don't make wine on the equator.

As important as temperature is sunlight which creates the process of photosynthesis that develops sugar in grapes. The reason why grapes ripen successfully in comparatively cool areas like Germany is that they have long sunny days at harvest time. Grapes will struggle to ripen even in a comparatively warm region if there isn't enough sun.

Rainfall/humidity Vines can't live without water but they can survive in a surprisingly dry climate. In fact, the more stressed they are and the more they dig down their roots to absorb nutrients from the mineral-rich subsoil, the better quality grapes they tend to produce. What winemakers ideally want is rain at the right time – during the winter and spring rather than in the middle of the harvest when it can damage the crop. Some degree of humidity is useful, particularly for the development of botrytis (the sought-after type of rot that afflicts grapes destined for dessert wines), but too much can lead to disease and less desirable types of rot.

Moderate climates Continental climates with hot summers and harsh winters can be harder to handle than more moderate maritime-influenced ones. In Washington State in northwestern America, for example, vines are damaged by the severe winter conditions about one year in six. In hot climates, on the other hand, some fluctuation between day and night temperatures is valuable, particularly for white wines – preserving freshness and adequate levels of acidity. Winemakers also ideally want to avoid an area that is regularly hit by strong winds or which is particularly susceptible to frost.

Vintage variations Regardless of the overall climate, weather conditions vary from one year to the next. This matters not just at harvest time, but in spring when the vines are budding and flowering. If the weather is unusually cold or wet, then not enough flowers will be fertilized and the number of berries per bunch will be reduced.

Most weather conditions are outside the wine producer's control, though surprisingly they can, given access to the right equipment, mitigate the effect of frost by the use of heaters, helicopters or wind machines which can agitate the air and prevent the temperature from falling below freezing. Sprinklers can also be used which protect the young shoots by covering them with a layer of ice. Heavy rain and hail are potentially far more serious, particularly near harvest time, as they can split the grapes and cause them to rot.

There tends to be less vintage variation in the New World than in regions which are at the margin of grape-growing viability, including classic European regions such as the Loire, Burgundy, and Germany. The effect is less disastrous in areas where the produce of one vintage is blended with those of previous years as in Champagne.

Above *Gravelly soil around Bordeaux reveals how superficially poor looking soil is often ideal for wine production forcing the vine to dig deep for moisture and nutrients.*

Far left *These neatly tended, widely spaced rows in California epitomize modern, large-scale, commercial vineyard practice. They have been specially laid out to facilitate as much mechanization as possible (both pruning and harvesting are often now done by machine).*

Choosing the best site

The ideal site for one style of wine may not necessarily be the best for another. If you intend to make a light, inexpensive, fruity wine for early consumption, you want a site that's easily managed, and gives the largest possible crop. If your ambitions are for a more serious wine, you'll want a vineyard that produces fewer grapes but much better quality ones.

Aspect Within many regions it is possible to find a particularly favourable microclimate – a range of hills that catches the rainfall so that it is usually dry the other side or, as in coastal areas such as California, cooling fogs or morning mists that roll in off the sea. Also important is the direction the vineyard faces. In cooler areas you want slopes that attract the maximum amount of sun.

The type of vineyard you have access to affects the kind of wine you can make. If you want to make a light, citrussy style of Chardonnay you'll need grapes grown on a cooler site and at a higher altitude than the warmer valley floor, where grapes with more tropical fruit flavours grow.

Soil The winemaker is not looking for highly fertile soil, as it can result in overproductive vines with too many leaves and poor quality grapes. The ideal soil is well drained but stores sufficient moisture within reach of the vine's deep-reaching roots. Some of the best vineyards, scattered with flat stones, look surprisingly inhospitable, but the stones can actually assist the ripening process by absorbing heat during the day, then reflecting it back on the vine at night.

There are certain distinctive soils which give the wine a particular flavour and character (referred to by the French as *goût de terroir*). Among them is the mineral-rich "terra rossa" soil of Coonawarra in South Australia, which lends a particularly intense quality to the Cabernet Sauvignon grown there. The ancient limestone and clay soil of Chablis helps to give the wine its steely, minerally quality.

Planting the right grapes

Having selected the vineyard, the producer then has to decide which type of grapes to grow in it. There is, for example, no point in planting a grape such as Shiraz (Syrah), that needs a hot climate to ripen properly, in Germany, or a grape such as Riesling, that needs a long, slow ripening period, in California's Central Valley. Some grapes such as Pinot Noir and Mourvèdre are notoriously difficult to handle and so would not be a viable choice if you could not expect to get a decent return for your wines.

Clones After selecting the grape variety, the producer chooses which clones or strains to plant. This decision is based on a variety of considerations, some commercial, some stylistic. Some clones promote higher yields; some are resistant to certain diseases. Others may be more typical of a style of wine that the producer wants to emulate, such as white or red burgundy. Often he or she only learns by trial and error which clones work best in the vineyards. Many producers in Oregon, for example, found that a Burgundian clone of Chardonnay was better suited to their comparatively cool climate than clones first imported from California, a much warmer wine region. For that reason, many winemakers hedge their bets and plant several different clones.

Rootstocks Since the re-appearance of phylloxera, the disease that wiped out much of the world's vineyards in the last century, many vines have been grafted onto indigenous American vine rootstocks resistant to the pest. Apart from giving immunity to the disease, the selection of a particular kind of rootstock is another tool that can be used to control or encourage the vine's vigour and adaptability to the soil.

Density How close or far apart you plant vines can determine how productive they are. In fertile conditions, planting vines close together means that they have to compete for the abundant nutrients available to them. In an arid, dry area you may want to give the plants a better chance of survival by planting them further apart. However, in many areas this decision is now more likely to rest on whether the vines are sufficiently spaced out to allow a mechanical harvester to pass through.

Age of vines The style of a wine can also be affected by the age of the vines. Younger vines, established for at least three years, tend to have an attractive fruitiness but little depth or complexity. Older vines of twenty to thirty years are generally less productive but create wines that are more intense. Most commercial wines come from grapes that are somewhere in between. Winemakers who use older vines usually highlight the fact on the label using the terms "Old Vine" or "Vieilles Vignes".

Above *This 100-year-old Shiraz vine, with its spectacularly gnarled trunk, is still very much in business as can be seen here. It may not produce many bunches, but the grapes should produce a wine with good concentration and complexity.*

Far left *These large, pale stones in the soil of this vineyard in Châteauneuf-du-Pape are known as pudding stones. They are vital to the ripening of the grapes as they retain the warmth from the sun and reflect it back up to the vines.*

Managing the vines

Left to themselves vines grow prolifically – a good thing, you might have thought – but what the wine producer wants is good quality grapes, not luxuriant vegetation. There are several ways of achieving this.

Training and trellising If you've travelled through a wine region, you will have seen the difference between the traditional "bush vine" and the typical modern vineyard with neat rows of elegantly trained vines. Good wine can be made from both, but winemakers prefer the more modern system of trellising, allowing them to prune and harvest mechanically, control disease, and control the vine's rigour. It also allows them to reposition vine shoots to ensure maximum exposure to the sun.

Pruning How drastically a vine should be pruned is open to argument, but most producers carry out some form of winter pruning to control the number of shoots, and consequently bunches of grapes, produced by the vine the following year. A summer pruning (*vendange verte*) can be carried out to further restrict the number of bunches or size of the yield.

More emphasis is now put on controlling the amount of leaves or "canopy" so that energy goes into the fruit rather than the leaves. By removing leaves or taking out shoots, a producer can affect the character of the wine. With Sauvignon Blanc, he or she can either accentuate the grassy, gooseberry character of the grapes by leaving them in the shade, or expose the grapes to the sun for riper, more tropical flavours.

Irrigating This is an emotive subject in Europe and is restricted or even forbidden in some areas. The argument is that too much watering dilutes the juice and increases the yield but most European vineyards enjoy an adequate level of rainfall. In some New World wine regions vines would die without irrigation and there need be no loss of quality with sophisticated modern drip irrigation systems that deliver precisely measured amounts of water to the vine.

Treatment/spraying Eradicating pests and diseases doesn't actually affect the style of the wine other than providing good raw materials to work on in the form of healthy grapes. The general trend is towards a more natural "green" approach, keeping the use of chemicals and fertilizers to a minimum and encouraging natural "cover crops" and insect populations to check disease and over-rapid growth instead.

Harvesting the grapes

Choosing the right moment to harvest is one of the most crucial decisions the wine-producer takes and the easiest to get wrong. If he or she picks before the grapes are fully ripe, the wine may suffer from sharp, acidic or green, herbaceous flavours. If the grapes are left on the vine too long they may lose their freshness and become overripe. And there's always the risk of a sudden storm blowing up which will spoil the crop entirely. Modern winemakers assess the state of their vineyards constantly, checking the ripeness of the grapes daily by appearance, taste, and chemical analysis.

Although the ideal harvesting time depends on the type of wine being made (for Champagne and sparkling wine it is better to pick grapes while they still have a high level of acidity), these days, producers are inclined to accept a higher level of risk and leave the grapes to ripen for as long as possible. A winemaker may in fact make a feature of this as in "Late-Picked" or "Late Harvest" dessert wines.

Machine or hand-picking   Although theoretically this is a choice, in reality, the decision to machine or hand pick depends on practical considerations. The main ones are whether the vineyards are designed for machine harvesting, whether there is a suitable pool of skilled labour to pick the grapes, and whether the regulations governing the region permit machine harvesting (in Champagne, for example, they don't).

Machine harvesting has the advantage of being quick, reliable, and relatively cheap – and harvesting can take place at night when the grapes are at their coolest. Hand harvesting, on the other hand, can be more precise and is vital where some kind of selection is required, for example, when picking grapes in a vineyard affected by botrytis. Most traditional estates in regions such as Bordeaux, Burgundy, and the Mosel still pick by hand, as do countries with a cheap labour force like South Africa and Chile. Australian grapes are mostly machine-picked.

Keeping the grapes cool   Next to deciding the right moment to pick, this is the most important aspect of harvesting. The danger of picking grapes in the heat of the day is that they will start to oxidize and lose their freshness, so most harvesting takes place in the early morning, if not at night. If there is a significant distance for the grapes to travel, they may well be transported to the winery in refrigerated trucks, or crushed in a temperature-controlled crushing station nearer the vineyard.

Above *Pickers at Château d'Yquem, Sauternes. Pickers may have to go through the vineyards as many a half a dozen times, each time selecting the grapes most affected by botrytis. This is the key to making fine late harvest wines and is time consuming, risky, and hugely expensive.*

Far left *These hoses running along the vines are for drip irrigation, illegal in most parts of Europe, but widely used in the hotter, drier parts of the New World. They can be computer controlled to give each vine precisely the right dose of water.*

WINEMAKING

If you walked into a large, modern winery you would be amazed; huge stainless-steel tanks run from floor to ceiling, encased in a network of ladders, hoses, and pumps. Banks of computerized controls monitor the temperature of each tank minute by minute. Fork-lift trucks bustle noisily around, moving barrels around cellars the size of a football pitch. It is a far cry from the romantic image of the small, French wine-producer with a couple of concrete tanks and a few barrels in a cobweb-festooned outhouse (though they still exist). Yet, fundamentally, wine is made in the same way from crushed grapes that are fermented into alcohol.

The big difference is in the amount of control that winemakers now have. For many small winemakers it used to be something of a hit and miss affair but now, within the limits of the fruit they have available, winemakers can more or less do what they want. They can control the fermentation temperature so that even in the hottest vine-growing areas you can make fresh fruity wine. They don't have to use expensive barrels to get oaky flavours, they can use chips or staves. They have access to sophisticated machines like ultra-gentle presses and filters which preserve rather than strip out flavour, and a battery of laboratory equipment to measure what they are doing at every stage.

How much of this bag of tricks a winemaker will employ depends on what part of the world he is operating in, how well-equipped his winery is, and how commercial a wine is being made. In some areas certain techniques are not permitted, for example the use of oak chips. With cheaper wines the aim is to produce a simple, fresh, fruity wine and bottle it as quickly as possible. With finer wines the winemaker has more time at his or her disposal and can allow processes to occur naturally rather than using chemicals to achieve them. For the winemaker it can often depend on the relatively mundane matter of how many tanks and barrels he or she has to play around with.

Like any other craftsmen, winemakers have their own ways of doing things. Some take more risks, allowing their wines to ferment at higher than average temperatures, using wild yeasts, and refusing to filter. Others are more inclined to play safe to ensure a consistent result.

Making white wine

The biggest and most obvious difference between white and red wine-making is colour. With white wines you don't want the juice to pick up colour from the skins so the grapes are pressed and the juice run off before fermentation rather than afterwards as with red wines. The winemaker's main objective is to preserve the grapes' natural fresh aromas and flavours – keeping the juice cool and protecting it from air. This is done partly physically by keeping it in a covered container and protecting it with a layer of carbon dioxide partly through the addition of sulphur dioxide and ascorbic acid which mop up the excess oxygen that can brown the grapes and dull their flavour.

The first step is to crush the grapes to release the juice. This is done as gently as possible so as not to split the pips which contain harsh woody flavours. (For the same reason the stems are normally removed.) This releases a certain amount of juice called the free-run juice which has a particularly pure fruit flavour and so may well be handled separately.

If the winemaker wants to extract extra body and flavour from the skins, he or she may leave the must (the mass of juice and skins) to soak for a couple of hours in the press or in a refrigerated tank for a few hours before pressing it. Again the press is likely to be designed to be as gentle as possible to avoid squeezing out harsh stalky flavours. The juice is then clarified either by filtering or settling (lowering the temperature so that the solids fall to the bottom of the tank), then pumped off into a holding tank or a fermentation tank. The object is to start the fermentation with the cleanest, freshest possible juice.

Which yeast? In order to get the fermentation started the winemaker needs to add yeast. In the past, wild yeasts that existed in the winery and on the skins of the grapes themselves were used, but these days most winemakers work with cultured yeasts (*i.e.* those grown in a laboratory). The advantage is not only that they are much more reliable and won't stop working halfway through, but that they can also accentuate certain fruity and floral aromas and flavours in the grapes.

Whether to chaptalize The addition of sugar or must concentrate (chaptalization) is done to boost the alcohol content of the grapes. It is routine in some regions such as northern Europe, but not permitted in others such as Australia.

Fermentation techniques In general, the fermentation temperatures are set at about 12–15°C (54–59°F) for simple, fresh, fruity whites and higher for fuller-bodied whites (18–20°C/65–68°F), allowing the development of more complex flavours. The juice may be simply fermented in stainless steel to retain its freshness. For fuller-bodied

*These are not perhaps the images you would expect of producers in Bordeaux (**above**) and Châteauneuf-du-Pape (**far left**), but they illustrate how much winemaking has moved away from the romantic images of barrels in dusty cellars. These small producers may still be in existence, but they are eclipsed by modern, well-equipped wineries which have greater control over their winemaking.*

styles, it may be fermented with oak chips or staves, or it could be barrel fermented – a technique that gives a particularly rich, creamy character. Alternatively, a combination of techniques will be used on different batches and the resulting wines blended together.

In the case of dry whites, the fermentation would be allowed to continue until all the sugar in the grapes had been converted to alcohol. If a slightly sweeter, medium-dry wine was required, the fermentation might be stopped, usually by the addition of sulphur dioxide, while some sugar was left in the grapes.

Malolactic fermentation This second fermentation, or "malo" as it is sometimes called, converts the harsher malic acids in the wine into softer lactic acids. It can either happen spontaneously or be induced by the addition of lactic bacteria. With most red wines it is allowed to take place, but with whites it is more of a conscious decision, depending on whether the winemaker wants to preserve a fresh, crisp edge to his wine or give it a richer, rounded, more buttery character.

Lees contact This is another way of enriching the flavour and texture of a wine. It involves leaving the wine on the lees, the spent yeast that has been used for fermentation, for several weeks. The lees may also be stirred from time to time to give the wine an even richer texture. Lees contact is often carried out as part of the barrel fermentation process, diminishing the harsher effects of new barrels.

Barrel maturation At least part of the blend (though not for fresh, crisp whites) may be either fermented in barrel or transferred to barrels after fermentation and aged for several weeks (*see* pages 32–3). Apart from the obvious effect of giving the wine a more oaky, toasty flavour, wood differs from stainless steel in that it keeps the wine at a higher temperature and allows an amount of oxidation, which leads to more complex flavours.

Fining and filtering With most fresh, fruity white wines, the wine would then simply be cleaned up before bottling. It would be chilled to precipitate tartrates (harmless but nonetheless slightly alarming-looking crystals that might otherwise appear in the bottle). Bentonite (a kind of clay) or other fining agents such as egg white or gelatine would then be added to attract the larger particles remaining in the wine. These would then fall to the bottom of the tank and be discarded when the wine was pumped off. Generally the wine will also be filtered, though winemakers now try to avoid excessive filtering as it strips out flavour. Further sulphur dioxide and sometimes ascorbic acid would be added to prevent the wine oxidizing or re-fermenting in the bottle.

The winemaker might also adjust the acidity and sweetness of the wine at this stage. If it was too sharp, it could be chemically de-acidified. If it needed to be sweeter, grape concentrate or juice could be added.

Blending options Much of the skill of the winemaker lies in using the components he or she has assembled to make a finished wine. Which ones are selected will depend on how many wines are being produced and at what kind of price. A large winery, for example, may produce several different wines for several different customers. A smaller estate may produce just two – a standard wine and a more expensive "reserve" wine. A typical mid-price New World Chardonnay, for example, will be a blend of about five or six components – thirty to forty per cent aged in oak, and the remainder treated with different yeasts and various levels of lees contact. The winemaker will make up several different blends from these components to see which works best before the wine is finally bottled and released.

Making red wine

The red-winemaker has different priorities from the white-winemaker. True, fresh fruit flavour is desirable, but the main concern is to get as much colour and flavour as possible from the skins. If the winemaker is seeking to make a wine that will last, he or she needs to get a base wine of sufficient intensity and concentration to support extended oak ageing.

In making a lighter red the main aim is to avoid excessive tannins so the grapes will be crushed and de-stemmed. Unlike white-winemaking, they then go straight into a fermentation tank – red wines are fermented with the grape skins present because that is where the colour lies.

Carbonic maceration The exception to this procedure is a technique called carbonic maceration. Instead of being crushed, whole grapes are left in a tank under a layer of carbon dioxide until they start to ferment. The effect is to give bright fruit flavours and soft tannins. The technique is used in Beaujolais but is also beneficial for grapes that can otherwise be very tough and tannic like Carignan.

Above *Punching down the "cap" of grape skins with long poles during fermentation helps release flavour and colour from the skins. If a wine does not have enough structure and flavour, it will not support much ageing in oak – it will be overwhelmed by it.*

Far left *In modern, hi-tech wineries such as Rosemount Estate in Australia, stainles-steel tanks are as common as oak barrels. Sophisticated, modern temperature control makes it possible to make fresh-tasting wines even in hot climates.*

Cold maceration This is another technique widely used by winemakers to create fruity wine with a deep colour without extracting harsh tannins. It involves soaking the crushed grapes in their own juice at a low temperature for anything from a week to three weeks.

Fermentation techniques Red wine fermentation starts in a similar way to that of whites. Yeast and possibly sugar or acid may be added (the former to boost the alcohol content, the latter to help preserve the colour and maintain a lively fruitiness). The grape must may also be warmed slightly to get the fermentation started and to help extract extra colour from the skins. The normal fermentation temperature for lighter reds is 22–26 °C (72–79 °F). For fuller-bodied wines, temperatures may be allowed to rise to 26–30 °C (79–86 °F) and even as high as 35 °C (95 °F).

As the fermentation takes off, the skins rise to the surface of the tank or container and have to be pushed back under the fermenting liquid, otherwise they will dry out and won't yield up their colour or flavour. This can be done manually or mechanically. Alternatives are to keep the cap (the skins) permanently submerged, circulate the liquid in the tank and pump it over the skins, or drain off the wine from the bottom of the tank and return it to the top.

The aim with a light fruity red would be to complete this process as quickly as possible so the juice is not left in contact with the skins for more than a few days. In other cases, a proportion of the wine might be drawn off before the fermentation has completed and then put into barrels to finish its fermentation. This results in better integration of the oak and fruit.

For more full-bodied wines the winemaker might leave a proportion of the fermented wine on the skins for a further period of three to four weeks before pressing to extract more flavour and colour. Another way of concentrating the juice is to run off a proportion of the juice after a limited amount of skin contact, which increases the ratio of skins to the remaining juice (the most common way of making rosé).

Pressing the juice Once the fermentation is complete, the winemaker will run off the juice, then put the remaining mass of grapes and skins through a press. This richer, more robust "press wine" may be returned to the rest of the juice to give it extra body. For high quality wines a proportion of the wine may be fermented from lightly crushed bunches or more rarely by treading the grapes by foot in the traditional way.

Oak ageing Lighter red wines are unlikely to be barrel-aged but, to make them more full-flavoured, a New World winemaker may age part of the blend in a tank with oak chips or staves or store them in an epoxy-lined concrete tank.

As with white wines, red wines can be aged in a variety of different types of wood (*see* pages 32–3). An important part of this process is racking, a device by which the wine is deliberately exposed to air by moving it from one barrel to another. It is a way of making the wine mature more quickly and also of avoiding the unpleasant sulphury smells that can accumulate if the wine is left in barrel for a long time. A fashionable alternative to racking, again used to soften tannins is "micro-oxygenation" which involves the release of controlled amounts of oxygen into a barrel or tank.

How long the wine spends in barrel – or maturing in the bottle – will depend on the price at which it is likely to be sold. Only producers of premium quality wines intended to last for several years (or those that are subject to regulations about the minimum age at which they can release their wines) are likely to age their wines for any length of time.

Fining and filtration Like white wines, light reds may be cold stabilized, and will simply be fined and filtered before bottling. A limited quantity of sulphur dioxide may also be added as a preservative.

Oak-ageing has a stabilizing and preservative effect, so that wines that have spent time in barrel don't generally need as much fining and filtering as those that haven't. Some winemakers make a feature of the fact that their wines are unfiltered on the basis that filtering diminishes a wine's intensity. Others believe that filtration technology has improved and that it is more important to have a stable, reliable product.

Tannin Any wine that is destined to last more than a couple of years needs a reasonable level of tannin – the preservative compound that is carried in the skins, stalks, and pips of the grapes – to hold it together. But judging the right amount can be tricky. Too little and the wine will soften too soon; too much and it can taste tough or dried out. Currently many winemakers eliminate the harsher tannins that come from the stalks by de-stemming and rely instead on the more subtle effects they can obtain from oak ageing. Tannin can also be added in powdered form at the fermentation stage.

Above *A modern bottling line such as this ensures that the wine is bottled as quickly and hygienically as possible. Wine faults in the past were often caused by clumsy, dirty bottling. Since wine is now officially regarded as a food, it is subject to much stricter hygiene controls.*

Far left *The finest wines will always spend some time ageing in oak barrels. They vary in size, but these 225-litre barriques made from new oak are the most popular. They are small enough to allow the wine to pick up the character of the oak.*

THE ROLE OF OAK

Many people have a strong opinion about whether or not oak in wine is a good thing. Their view is often based on their experience of notably oaky wines such as Californian Chardonnay or Spanish Rioja. But the issue is not as black and white as it might at first appear.

Originally wood had a perfectly straightforward function in relation to wine – that of a watertight container for storage and transport. Over the years winemakers have discovered that storage in wood not only has the bonus of naturally clarifying and stabilizing wine, but can also affect its character by adding complex layers of flavour to white wines and greater longevity and structure to reds. The degree to which this happens depends on a number of factors.

Extent and manner of oak contact Wine can be stored in small barrels (in which case the oak influence will be more dominant) or in large oak casks. Alternatively, oak chips can be added to the wine during fermentation, either loose or encased in fabric like an oversized tea bag. A winemaker can also insert wooden staves inside a tank to give a similar effect.

Age of the container The barrels could be brand new or have been used only once or twice before. If an old oak cask is being used, its wood influence will be negligible. As you would expect, the newer the wood, the more powerful the oak flavour.

Type of oak Tight-grained French oak is still considered superior to any other kind of oak, as it has a more subtle influence on the wine than barrels which are made from Eastern European or American oak. The latter is used for full-bodied reds such as Australian Shiraz and Rioja.

Degree of "toast" This is the extent to which the cooper (barrel-maker) chars or "toasts" the inside of the barrel. A moderate degree of toast will modify crude oak flavours.

Length of time in oak How long the wine spends in contact with oak – a few months or over a year. Whether the wine is actually fermented in the barrel is also significant. This technique is favoured for more expensive white wines, as it gives them an opulent creamy texture and helps integrate the oak flavours, but is increasingly used for reds too.

Maturity of the wine when consumed Even with very oaky wines the influence of oak diminishes over time and the harsh tannins soften.

As important as any of these factors is the role of the winemaker. Certainly, wines of any quality will be assembled from several components which may come from different vineyards and be aged in different kinds of oak for varying lengths of time. Part of the blend may, in fact, not have had any oak contact at all, but will have been aged in neutral stainless steel to accentuate its natural fruit.

With oak, as with other aspects of wine, you generally get what you pay for. A white wine, for instance, costing £4–5 a bottle is going to show a much cruder oak influence than a fine burgundy matured in barrels made by a leading French cooper. Oak chips cost about one tenth of the £400–450 a winemaker pays for a standard 225-litre French oak barrel (this is not an unreasonable price when you consider that the wood is cut from trees that are at least eighty years old and may be seasoned for another two years before the cooper can use it). Although the quality of oak chips or, more recently, oak staves, can give a pleasant effect, they are never going to achieve the sublimely creamy texture of wine aged in the best new oak barrels.

The fashion now is for far less overt oak character than was popular in the 1980s and 1990s. Winemakers are concentrating more on achieving balanced, integrated flavours with increased subtlety.

Oaked or unoaked?

Not all wines that are matured in oak taste obviously oaky. Most wines that are kept in old oak casks, including many fine white wines from Germany and Alsace, show no obvious flavour of the wood. Conversely, some wines, such as Semillons from Australia and traditionally made full-bodied reds from the south of France, including Fitou, appear to be oaked when they haven't been anywhere near a barrel.

What to look for on the label

As oak is expensive, winemakers who use it tend to boast about it. Descriptions such as "barrel-matured" or "barrel-fermented", "*elevé en fûts de chêne*" or the term "*reserva*" or "*gran reserva*" indicate a significant oak influence. The back label may tell you how long the wine has been kept in oak, whether the oak is French or American, and how new the barrels are. Terms like "oak-influenced" or "oak character" generally indicate the use of chips or staves rather than barrels.

Above *A cooper "toasting" the staves of oak. This process, which helps bend the staves into the right shape, ultimately has a powerful effect on the flavour of the wine.*

Far left *The spectacular sight of a barrel cellar. The extensive financial investment involved in ageing wines in barrels inevitably results in some very expensive wines.*

WINE STYLES EXPLAINED

Over the next sixty-eight pages you'll find the heart of the book, the descriptions of the main wine styles. There are four white (crisp fresh dry; smooth, medium-bodied; rich, full-bodied; and aromatic and medium-dry) and four red (light fruity; smooth, medium-bodied; full-bodied; and aged wines and rarities). There are also sections for rosé, sparkling, sweet, and fortified wines (sherry, port, and madeira). In each section you'll find an extensive listing of wines fitting that description. Each section is prefaced by an introduction highlighting the most interesting wines in that style.

Start with the style of wine you like best, for example crisp dry whites. Against each entry you'll find a series of symbols which tell you at a glance the main flavours in that wine, such as grassy, fruity, and minerally. These are listed in order so that you can tell which flavour dominates. You'll also find these symbols next to other wines in other sections so if you like, for instance, spicy or oaky wines, you'll be able to pick them out all the way through the book. Keys are provided below and on the back cover of the book.

Also marked against each entry is a star rating, which indicates the likely cost of the wine. It ranges from one star, which is the least expensive, to three stars, which is the dearest. Bear in mind that these are relative to the type of wine. A one star light, fruity red, for instance, will be a simple quaffing wine. A single star for Champagne means it is inexpensive for Champagne but obviously that doesn't make it cheap.

In most of the style sections you'll find a box headed **Starting Points**. These are suggestions of wines that you might like to try if you haven't drunk that type of wine before. They tend to be the most typical

Key to symbols

- Fruity
- Floral
- Minerally
- Spicy
- Nutty
- Grassy
- Toasty
- Oaky

| Crisp, fresh, dry whites | Smooth, medium-bodied whites | Rich, full-bodied whites | Aromatic and medium-dry whites |

examples of that wine style, but they're also divided up to reflect the different options open to you. For example, in the aromatic whites section you can decide whether to experiment first with wines that are light and floral, fragrant and spicy or rich and aromatic.

There's also a section called **Label Clues**. These point out the key information you should look for on a label, such as references to the presence or absence of oak, the alcohol content (always a useful clue to a wine's body and intensity) and the vintage.

By the side of the listings you'll find advice about storing and serving that particular style of wine, including how long you should keep it, how long you should open it before you drink it, what temperature you should serve it at, and (where appropriate) the type of glasses you should serve it in. You'll find more general advice about storing and serving on pages 110–13. There's also an indication of the type of food and occasion for which that style of wine is most appropriate – or inappropriate. Again, you'll find more advice about matching food and wine in the section on Wine and Food (*see* pages 104–9).

As you go through the book don't be surprised to find a wine in more than one section. Red burgundy, for example, can at its most basic be light and fruity, most is medium-bodied, while expensive top burgundies such as Gevrey-Chambertin and Nuits-St-Georges count as full-bodied, and *grands crus* such as Romanée-Conti come into the category of aged wines and rarities. By and large, you will find these distinctions reflected in the price you pay. The more expensive the wine, the more intense and full-bodied it generally is.

There are always exceptions to the rule. Some wines may differ slightly from their general descriptions in the listings. That's inevitable, because wine as a product is hugely varied. As in any other profession, some winemakers are better at their job than others, or have better grapes to work with and a more reliable climate to work in. Wines inevitably vary between one producer and the next. You may initially find this frustrating, but discovering the unexpected and delightful wine is one of the great pleasures of wine drinking and what makes it so memorable!

| Light, fruity reds | Smooth, medium-bodied reds | Full-bodied reds | Aged wines and rarities | Rosé wines |

CRISP, FRESH, DRY WHITES

Dry is a troublesome word in wine terms, for what is dry to one person may well not be so to another. For people accustomed to the tropical fruit of Australian and Californian Chardonnay, Chablis would seem very dry. For someone brought up on Muscadet, it would taste quite rich.

Nevertheless, there is a group of wines that ranges from bone dry whites such as Muscadet and Pinot Grigio to zesty New World Sauvignon that really couldn't be described as anything but dry. What these have in common is a crisp, tangy acidity that is in marked contrast to the smoother, rounded flavours of a Chardonnay or a wine made with oak.

Virtually all basic dry whites fall into this category, apart from those Germanic-style whites that have a distinctively floral, aromatic character (see page 54). The simple kind of quaffing wine you drink on holiday, the carafe wine in a restaurant, the cheapest whites on a supermarket shelf – all tend to be light, crisp, uncomplicated, and fruity.

Most of them come from the Old World rather than the New. Hot climates tend to bring out richer, fruitier flavours than wines made in cooler more northerly regions. You would not find a wine like Muscadet or Vinho Verde in Australia. Chablis which is grown at virtually the same northerly latitude as the vineyards of the Loire has an altogether different character from a Chardonnay made in the Hunter Valley.

The style of many of these wines dates from when winemaking was much less sophisticated. Winemakers would use whatever local grapes were available and get the highest yields possible out of them, fashioning them in the most rudimentary way into simple quaffing wines that would be drunk on an everyday basis. In Italy, for example, local white wines such as Orvieto in Umbria and Frascati in Rome are still drunk with almost every kind of food, from pasta dishes right through to robustly flavoured stews.

Clean, modern wines

What has revolutionized this style of wine is modern vinification. It used to be impossible to make a fresh wine in a hot climate; the grapes would get too hot and the fermentation would take place at high temperatures producing yellow, oxidized wines. Now wines are made in immaculately clean, temperature-controlled stainless-steel tanks. Almost any wine can be made to taste fresh, zesty, and invigorating.

The most characterful wines in this style are undoubtedly those made from the Sauvignon Blanc grape which, like Chardonnay, has spread from its traditional base in France to almost every wine-producing country in the world. Its style varies markedly from the refined, steely Sauvignons of the Loire to the intense gooseberry and tropical fruit of those from New Zealand's Marlborough region (*see also* page 57).

If you find such robust flavours not to your taste, there are plenty of alternatives. Refreshing Italian whites such as Pinot Grigio and Frascati, the wonderfully seafood-friendly Albariño or the intruiguing peppery flavour of an Austrian Grüner Veltliner can all provide a refreshing antidote to the sometimes over-exuberant ripe fruitiness of many New World wines.

One crucial thing to remember is that this type of crisp, fresh fruit fades fast. With the exception of the more expensive Sauvignons and Chablis, the vast majority of bottles made in this style should be drunk as young as possible, within twelve months and in the case of cheaper wines within six. (Remember that southern hemisphere whites are six months ahead of European ones, typically arriving on the shelf in the autumn of the year they are harvested rather than the following spring.)

Label clues

"Dry White" should be an indication that a wine is precisely that, but sometimes wines labelled "dry" have an unexpectedly floral character. Check the back label for descriptions such as fragrant or aromatic (as opposed to crisp, fruity or citrussy). Wines that are described simply as "*blanc*" (France), "*bianco*" (Italy), "*blanco*" (Spain), or "*branco*" (Portugal) generally offer simple, fresh easy drinking.

Check the alcohol content of the wine – if you prefer a lighter style, look for wines of under twelve degrees.

Starting points	
Minerally	**Fruity**
Pinot Grigio	Vin de Pays des Côtes de Gascogne
Muscadet	Inexpensive Sauvignons from France and Chile
Unoaked Chablis	South African Sauvignon Blanc
Sancerre	

Above *The distinctively gnarled, low-lying Assyrtiko vines of Santorini's volcanic vineyards produce some of the world's most individual and pure-tasting white wines.*

Far left *The cool, high altitudes of much of northern Italy result in elegant, fresh flavours in the white wines.*

ALBARINO

Elegant dry white from the Galicia region of northwest Spain that finds its way into many smart restaurants' winelists. Excellent with seafood. ☆☆

ALIGOTE

Burgundy's lesser known white wine grape Aligoté produces wines that can taste uncomfortably sharp which is why it is the wine most often used to make a kir. But better examples can be attractively fresh and crisp – like lesser Chablis. ☆

ASSYRTIKO

Intensely sharp, delicious lemony white, the best of Greece's new wave whites. ☆☆

BACCHUS, ORTEGA, and other English whites

In the past English whites were made in a medium-dry style. But better quality grape varieties like Bacchus, Ortega, and Reichensteiner, which are suited to the English climate, have made it possible to produce fresh, crisp dry whites similar to French Sauvignon Blanc in style but with more of a flowery, sometimes elderflower character. ☆☆

BADEN and other dry German whites

One of the warmer regions of Germany, Baden also gives its name to an attractive dry wine, quite distinctive from the majority of German whites. Other dry whites such as Weissburgunder (Pinot Blanc) and Grauburgunder (Pinot Gris) are becoming increasingly popular. ☆☆

BAIRRADA

The best-known Portuguese white after VINHO VERDE is a fresh, crisp, citrussy white. Cheaper versions are quite lemony, more expensive wines, more elegant and minerally. ☆→☆☆

BIANCO DI CUSTOZA

Light, dry white from the Veneto in northeast Italy: clean and crisp with a touch of creaminess, but generally rather less exciting than neighbouring SOAVE. ☆→☆☆

BORDEAUX, DRY WHITE, UNOAKED

Basic dry white Bordeaux from appellations such as Entre-Deux-Mers has greatly improved in quality over recent years, producing simple, attractive lemony whites. Much is based on Sauvignon Blanc though some also include some Semillon and Muscadelle. ☆

CHABLIS

The best known example of dry, crisp Chardonnay. Grand and premier cru Chablis may be more full-bodied, but simple unoaked Chablis and **Petit Chablis** have a characteristically austere steely character, often evocatively described as flinty. ☆☆

CHARDONNAY

This grape variety falls firmly within the next two style sections, but there are exceptions. Some white burgundies, notably those from younger vines, from a particularly cool area, or which are unoaked, can taste quite tart and crisp. (*see* CHABLIS)

Any other Chardonnay grown in cool conditions will exhibit a similar character. For example there are a number of inexpensive Chardonnays produced in the Loire now under the label of **Vin de Pays du Jardin de la France**. They may be less lean than Chablis but they are crisp rather than smooth. ☆→☆☆

CHASSELAS

Swiss grape variety used for bone dry white wines that are good with cooked cheese dishes like fondue. Rarely seen outside Switzerland, but certainly the wine to drink there. ☆☆

CHENIN BLANC – Loire Valley

Although Chenin Blanc can acquire rich, honeyed tones with age, young Chenin, particularly in the cool Loire Valley in France, is often quite sharp. Quality varies from the rather dull wines of **Anjou** and **Saumur** (also made in medium-dry versions – *see* pages 54–9) to the austere, minerally elegance of **Savennières** and **Jasnières**. ☆→☆☆☆

FRASCATI

 The famous dry white wine of Rome, Frascati often used to be light and dilute. Those that find their way outside Italy these days are usually much fuller and fruitier. ☆→☆☆

GARGANEGA

 The grape that is used to make Soave and Bianco di Custoza sometimes stars on its own. More characterful than TREBBIANO, with a delicate almond flavour. ☆

GRUNER VELTLINER

 This indigenous Austrian grape variety has become increasingly popular over the last few years. Younger wines tend to have a distinctive fresh green and white pepper flavour like Riesling. Also like Riesling, better quality wines can acquire more complex spicy, aromatic flavours over time (see pages 54–9). ☆→☆☆☆

MUSCADET

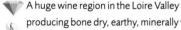 A huge wine region in the Loire Valley producing bone dry, earthy, minerally whites that at their best are elegant, crisp, and refreshing, at their worst, painfully thin and acidic. The best wines tend to be those from the Sèvre-et-Maine part of the region and are labelled "sur lie". They have a richer, nuttier flavour. A similar style of wine, also from this region, is **Gros Plant**. ☆→☆☆

ORVIETO

 A lesser-known Italian white, from Umbria in central Italy. Orvieto is clean and crisp with an appealing, slightly earthy, nutty character, particularly in the higher-quality "Classico" wines. "Amabile" wines are a little sweeter. ☆→☆☆

PICPOUL DE PINET and other southern French whites

 This is a crisp, fresh, minerally Muscadet-style white produced from the Picpoul grape on the Languedoc coast in southern France. Other inexpensive whites in a similar style are produced in the area from grapes such as Grenache Blanc, Terret, and Vermentino. ☆

PINOT BIANCO

 The Italian name both for the Pinot Blanc grape and the wine made from it, mainly in the northeast of the country. It tends to be crisper and more acidic than French Pinot Blanc. ☆

PINOT GRIGIO

 An increasingly fashionable grape variety, particularly in the USA, grown mainly in northeast Italy where it produces characteristically dry, crisp, neutral-tasting whites. Some winemakers now produce wines with a more pronounced fruit character, though they are never as rich or aromatic as wines labelled Pinot Gris (the alternative name of the grape). ☆→☆☆

Food and occasions

Crisp, fresh, whites are ideal for straightforward, everyday drinking, especially summer picnics and parties. They are perfect for drinking with salads or with grilled or barbecued fish and chicken. Muscadet has a great affinity with shellfish, while Chablis is the traditional partner for oysters. Italian whites are good with pasta, particularly made with seafood. Fruitier styles like Sauvignon go well with robustly flavoured fish dishes, chicken, and piquantly dressed salads. Delicate Loire Sauvignons work particularly well with asparagus, smoked salmon, and goat's cheese while New Zealand Sauvignon is wonderful with Thai food.

RIESLING, young dry

While most dry Riesling acquires an aromatic or floral character with age, very young Riesling, especially from Alsace, is crisp and dry with marked green apple and citrus flavours. ☆→☆☆☆

RIOJA, unoaked

White Rioja used to taste heavily oaked from being left for months in oak barrels. Now a lighter, fresher style is popular. Most are made from the Viura grape: light and fresh when unoaked, rounded, creamy, and more Chardonnay-like when oaked. ☆→☆☆

RUEDA

One of Spain's most progressive wine regions which also gives its name to a crisp, fresh style of white based on the local Verdejo grape variety (often blended with Sauvignon thrown in). Excellent value for money. ☆

SANCERRE & POUILLY-FUME

The best-known SAUVIGNONS from the Loire region in France, Sancerre and Pouilly-Fumé combine the characteristic gooseberry fruit with a pronounced grassiness, an aroma of currant leaves, and a distinctive flinty, almost smoky character. They can also be quite acidic, particularly in a difficult vintage. More expensive wines from top producers such as Dagueneau may receive some oak ageing and belong in the full-bodied category (*see* pages 48–53). ☆☆→☆☆☆☆

SAUVIGNON BLANC

The Loire As with so many other wines, French Sauvignon provides the benchmark for the variety around the world. Its most distinctive manifestations are the elegant grassy gooseberryish wines from this region, notably SANCERRE and POUILLY-FUME, and the lesser known **Menetou-Salon**, **Quincy**, and **Reuilly**, cheaper **Sauvignon de Touraine** and **Sauvignon de Haut-Poitou**. ☆→☆☆☆

Bordeaux Sauvignon from this region and surrounding areas tends to be more citrussy and is often combined with Semillon which gives it a roundness and softness that takes it out of this category. But crisp, fresh whites are produced by appellations such as ENTRE-DEUX-MERS, **Bergerac**, **Côtes de Duras,** and simply as basic **Bordeaux Blanc**. ☆→☆☆

Languedoc Sauvignon is also widely planted throughout the Languedoc, a warmer region which gives it a richer, lime and lemon peel character. It is often produced as a varietal *vin de pays* (under the classification **Vin de Pays d'Oc**) and has more of a New World character than other French Sauvignons. ☆→☆☆

Other European Sauvignon No other European country produces such distinctive styles of Sauvignon as France, but most can boast one or two good examples. In Italy the most successful area for Sauvignon is Friuli in the northeast. In Spain it's RUEDA. In Austria, Styria. The large number of "flying winemakers" who have been working in Hungary has resulted in some powerfully flavoured wines, not subtle, but remarkable value for money. ☆→☆☆

New Zealand Sauvignon is the grape that has made New Zealand's reputation, and, indeed, the pungent version of the wine that it produces, with its rich gooseberry and tropical fruit, is as good as you'll find anywhere in the world. Many are so intense that they should more accurately be regarded as aromatic, though the chances are that if you enjoy other New World Sauvignons, you will also enjoy New Zealand's. The best examples come from the Marlborough region to the north of the South Island. They tend to be expensive, but are consistently reliable. ☆☆→☆☆☆

South Africa The style of South African Sauvignon tends to be midway between those of France and New Zealand. The best examples from cool regions such as Constantia rank among the world's finest. ☆→☆☆☆

Chile Sauvignon from here tends to be softer and less pungent than that from New Zealand, with a more pronounced citrus, especially grapefruit character. The best wines come from the Casablanca Valley, a well-favoured, cool, coastal region which produces wines of considerable elegance and style. ☆→☆☆☆

California Californians actually prefer their Sauvignon softer and less grassy, hence the popularity of Fumé Blanc (*see* pages 42–7). But there are Sauvignons made in the more typical crisp, citrussy style. If you prefer that style look out for wines that are labelled Sauvignon rather than Fumé Blanc. ☆☆

Australia Although a bit hot to be ideal Sauvignon growing territory, Australia does have producers who do so successfully, particularly in cooler areas such as the Adelaide Hills. The resulting wines tend to be quite intensely flavoured, often with a pronounced lemon peel character. ☆☆

SAVENNIERES

 Bone dry Chenin Blanc from the Loire which, like other top Chenin, can age for many years. ☆☆→☆☆☆

SOAVE

 Another very much improved wine from the Veneto in northeast Italy. You still find some dreary examples about, but at its best, Soave has a distinctive, delicate almondy flavour that makes it an attractive partner for food. Wines labelled "Classico" could equally well fall into the next section (see pages 42–7). ☆→☆☆

VERDICCHIO DEI CASTELLI DI JESI

 The best-known wine made from the Verdicchio grape, this romantic sounding wine from the eastern side of Italy has an attractively fresh, tangy, slightly lemony flavour. It frequently comes in a distinctive, curvy bottle. ☆→☆☆

VERMENTINO

 Yet another crisp, fresh citrussy, slightly earthy Italian white. Some of the best examples come from Sardinia. It is also widely planted in Corsica and provides some attractive wines in the Languedoc where it is known as Rolle. ☆☆

VERNACCIA DI SAN GIMIGNANO

 Made around the famous hillside town just outside Florence from the local Vernacchia grape. Like VERDICCHIO, it still tends to be made the traditional way, resulting in a crisp fresh white not unlike a MUSCADET. ☆→☆☆

VIN DE PAYS DES COTES DE GASCOGNE

 One of the first French vins de pays to gain widespread popularity, Vin de Pays des Côtes de Gascogne, which comes from southwest France, provides fresh, fruity, uncomplicated drinking. A vin de pays is almost always a better buy than a simple vin blanc. ☆→☆☆

VINHO VERDE

 Portugal's best-known white wine. Most is very light in alcohol, quite sharp, and with a slight spritz: the kind of wine you enjoy on holiday, but which doesn't always translate into good drinking back home. Estate-bottled versions are more interesting, particularly those made from the Alvarinho grape. ☆→☆☆

Storing and serving

Serve chilled (at least an hour in the fridge). Drink as soon as possible after you buy it, within six months for cheaper wines and two years for the best wines in this category.

SMOOTH, MEDIUM-BODIED DRY WHITES

If someone wanted to learn about wine and asked you where they should start, you'd probably point them to a smooth, dry white. Not too sharp or acidic, not too intimidatingly oaky, not too floral or sweet, white wine like this is the perfect starting point for your exploration of the wine world.

The chances are you wouldn't direct them to just any smooth, dry white wine, you'd pour them a glass of Chardonnay. Chardonnay is the wine that dominates this section more than any other. It's the one you'll find most often on the supermarket shelf, the one you'll find in restaurants. There is literally a world of Chardonnay to choose from.

So what distinguishes Chardonnay that is made in this style from the more fuller-flavoured kind? As is explained earlier in the book, it's primarily a question of the climate the vines are grown in and whether or not the resulting wine is oaked (see pages 32–3). On the whole you'll find that Chardonnay grown in cooler, more northerly regions such as Burgundy and northern Italy, or in cooler parts of warmer countries like Chile, will be lighter and creamier than Chardonnay produced in hot countries such as Australia or South Africa or warmer areas such as the Languedoc in the south of France.

Subtle use of oak

Chardonnay made in this style may well be oaked, but it doesn't have the obvious oaky character of, say, a top California Chardonnay or an expensive white burgundy. Apart from the inherent quality of the grapes themselves, this subtlety could be due to the fact that the wine is not made in brand new oak barrels, that the barrels are made out of French rather than American oak, or that it only spends a relatively short time in barrel or in contact with oak chips or staves (see pages 32–3). Even wines made in this style vary. Ageing a small proportion of the wine in oak (ten or fifteen per cent) will give it a smoother, richer character than unoaked Chardonnay.

In the absence of obvious clues from the winemaker, such as putting "barrel-fermented" on the label, the best guide to style is price. Most inexpensive or moderately priced Chardonnays will be lighter and fruitier in style than expensive ones. This is particularly apparent among wines made by the world's biggest wine-producing companies. However, the rule is not a hard and fast one because producers in countries with low production costs, such as Argentina, Chile or South Africa, may produce a big oaky wine that is comparatively cheap.

Well-known brands that sell to literally hundreds of thousands of people are deliberately made in a smoothly fruity, easy-drinking style.

Chardonnay apart, where else within this style should you pursue your wine drinking adventures? Well, it depends on your personal preference. If you like a lighter, more creamy style of wine you should try something like a South African Chenin Blanc or the delicately peachy flavours of a New Zealand or Oregon Pinot Gris. If you prefer something slightly sweeter-tasting you might consider a Colombard or the classic Australian blend of Semillon and Chardonnay with its exuberant, ripe pineapple fruit.

If you're looking for more distinctive flavours you're more likely to find them in the Old World. White oaked Bordeaux, which is much less well-known than its red counterpart, offers beautifully elegant drinking and can be a good choice on wine lists. Alsace Pinot Blanc is an underrated treasure. Italy has more to offer than the simple Frascatis and Pinot Grigio you find in the typical *trattoria*. Show you're in the know by ordering a peachy Fiano or smooth, creamy Lugana.

Finally, don't make the mistake of thinking that just because these wines are slightly more expensive than the simple, everyday quaffing wines that were described in the last section, you can store them away for years. Almost all modern wines now are meant to be drunk young and this style of wine is no exception.

Label clues

Scan the back label for clues about how the wine is made. Expressions like "lightly oaked" or "left on its lees" indicate a lighter style. Mention of "barrel fermentation" or "up to a year in oak" means the wine belongs in the next section. Look out for an alcohol content of 12.5–13.5 per cent ABV .

Above *Chile's cool, coastal-influenced Casablanca Valley has acquired a reputation for its crisp, citrussy Chardonnays.*

Far left *Bordeaux produces some of the finest examples of this style. The best wines are lush and smooth and have a delicious subtle peachiness.*

Starting points	
Drier	**Fruitier**
Inexpensive or moderately priced white burgundy	Unoaked Australian Chardonnay
Alsace Pinot Blanc	Chardonnay
South African Chenin Blanc	Semillon/Chardonnay
Chilean Chardonnay	New World Colombard
	Vin de Pays d'Oc
	Viognier

BORDEAUX BLANC

While basic white Bordeaux is simple, crisp, and fruity, wines from this region that are oaked take on a much more lush, smooth, peachy quality. This is mainly due to the fact that they are not pure Sauvignon Blanc but a blend of Sauvignon and SEMILLON (and occasionally Muscadelle) and Semillon has a particular affinity with oak. The best known white Bordeaux is **Graves** – though the top quality wines now come from the breakaway appellation of **Pessac-Léognan** (*see* pages 48–53). ☆☆→☆☆☆

BOURGOGNE BLANC

Basic white burgundy (Appellation Bourgogne Blanc) is highly variable in quality. At its worst it can be dull and characterless, but at its best it is attractively light and creamy. Producers who also include the word Chardonnay on the label are likely to make their wine in a more typically fruity New World style. ☆☆

BURGUNDY

White burgundy in general has a quite distinctive character that traditionally has little in common with New World CHARDONNAY, though several producers are now making their wines in a more obviously New World style. The fruit flavours are much less obvious, peach or apricot rather than mango and pawpaw, but above all, the feel of the wine in your mouth is different. There's a creamy, slightly oily texture and savouriness about burgundy that you rarely find anywhere else

and which becomes more pronounced as the wine gets older. (Unlike most inexpensive and medium priced New World Chardonnays, white burgundy will age for several years.)

Most of the wines in this price range and style come from the Mâconnais and Côte Chalonnaise regions (MACON and MONTAGNY), rather than the more prestigious Côte de Beaune (*see* pages 48–53). Wines that are made by individual growers, even given quite humble labels like BOURGOGNE BLANC, are generally better quality than wines from the big *négociants* and cooperatives. ☆☆→☆☆☆

CHABLIS

Although Chablis, which is to the north of the BURGUNDY region is traditionally steely-dry (*see* pages 36–41) the region's producers are increasingly responding to the demand from wine-drinkers for smoother, less acidic wines. Much standard Chablis is now made in this style, though wines labelled Premier or Grand Cru (which, unlike most basic Chablis, are often aged in oak) will be more full-bodied (*see* pages 48–53). ☆☆→☆☆☆

CHARDONNAY

Bulgaria, Hungary, and Moldova Flying

winemakers are much in evidence in this part of the world producing simple, smooth, lightly oaked Chardonnays that offer exceptionally good value for money. Wines that are described as barrel- or barrique-fermented will be fuller-bodied. ☆

Italy Most Italian Chardonnay is produced in the northeast of country in the Alto Adige,

Trentino, Fruili, and the Veneto. When unoaked it tends to be quite light, crisp, and lemony; when oaked much like mid-price Chardonnay from any other cool wine region. Names to look out for are **Chardonnay delle Venezie** (or Tre Venezie), **Chardonnay del Trentino**, and **Chardonnay del Piemonte**. For a fuller style try **Chardonnays** from Puglia and Sicily down in the south. ☆→☆☆

New World Chardonnay Most moderately

priced New World Chardonnay is made in a smooth, medium-bodied style. The difference between them lies in how fruity or how oaky they are. The lighter, more citrussy ones tend to come from Chile, the more fruity from South Africa or Australia, the oakiest from California and Argentina. More expensive bottles from Australia and South Africa are generally made in a fuller style. Wines to look out for are the increasingly popular unoaked or unwooded Chardonnays which tend to have a particularly fresh peachy or melony flavour without the marked oak character that some drinkers find unappealing. ☆→☆☆

Pays d'Oc Chardonnay The huge sprawling

Languedoc region in the south of France has become a playground for overseas (particularly Australian) winemakers and many of the Chardonnays from the region reflect that fruitier New World style. That is especially likely with wines that are given anglicised names, or where the name Chardonnay is prominent on the label: usually alongside the appellation Vin de Pays d'Oc. Chardonnay produced around the cooler Limoux region to the north of the Languedoc is generally creamier and more Burgundian in style. ☆→☆☆

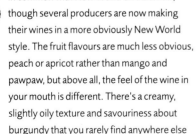

CHARDONNAY BLENDS

 Blends of Chardonnay with other grape varieties are common to reduce the cost of the wine. The style varies depending on which grape it is blended with. Blends with less expensive varieties such as CHENIN BLANC or VIURA tend to result in lighter wines. Blends with varieties with a more dominant personality like COLOMBARD and SEMILLON will produce much fruitier, fuller-flavoured wines. ☆→☆☆

CHENIN BLANC

 Chenin grown in the New World tends not to have the same tart acidity as that from the Loire Valley in France. Most comes from South Africa where it produces smooth, melony whites, often with a touch of sweetness. Some winemakers, though, are experimenting with barrel-fermentation or leaving the young wine on its lees, resulting in wines with a fuller, creamier texture. Wines that come from older vines also tend to be rather more stylish and elegant.

Chenin is also quite widely grown by wine producers in California, Chile, and Argentina with similar results. Blends with other grapes such as CHARDONNAY, Sauvignon, and COLOMBARD take on the characteristics of those more dominant varieties. ☆→☆☆

COLOMBARD

 Australian Colombard has a particularly ripe, tropical fruity character that can make it easily mistaken for CHARDONNAY – with which it is often blended. But it doesn't quite have Chardonnay's subtlety of flavour or smooth creamy texture and can frequently taste almost sweet. It is also widely planted in South Africa where it is used to make inexpensive fruity whites, again often blended with Chardonnay or CHENIN BLANC. ☆

COTES DU RHONE

 White Côtes du Rhône is much less well-known than red, but is increasingly producing attractively fresh fruity whites that can make a refreshing change from New World varietals. ☆→☆☆

FIANO

 Attractive, smooth, peachy Chardonnay-like white originally from the Campania region of Southern Italy but also planted in Sicily. ☆→☆☆

FUME BLANC

 Fumé Blanc was an ingenious name cooked up by the California wine producer Robert Mondavi for Sauvignon Blanc, whose green herbaceous flavours were initially not popular with Californians. Despite the increased popularity of Sauvignon Blanc it retains a following. It is generally lightly oaked and therefore softer, less acidic, and more appley than French or other New World Sauvignons. ☆→☆☆

Food and occasions

This style of wine is infinitely adaptable: it goes with a wide range of different dishes and fits into almost any occasion. Lighter styles go well with fish, chicken, and pasta, particularly if accompanied by a creamy sauce. A good quality wine like a white burgundy will accompany rich fish like salmon or a classic roast chicken. Fruitier styles can take slightly spicier flavours. A good style of wine for informal entertaining.

GAILLAC

 A soft, spicy, slightly appley white from the southwest of France made from the local Mauzac grape variety. ☆

GAVI DI GAVI

 Stylish, elegant, dry white wine from the Piedmont region of northern Italy whose price can be out of proportion to its quality. A better bargain can be wines labelled **Cortese** which is the grape that is used to make Gavi. ☆☆ → ☆☆☆

GREEK OAKED WHITES

 Many of Greece's most exciting winemakers are producing deliciously lush smooth wines from oak-aged varieties such as Assyrtiko. ☆☆

LUGANA

 Another stylish and occasionally pricey Italian white from Lombardy to the south of Lake Garda in northern Italy, with a creamy, delicately nutty, subtle flavour. Similar in style to a good quality SOAVE CLASSICO. ☆☆

MACON-VILLAGES

 Wines from the Mâconnais region to the north of Beaujolais are generally fuller flavoured than CHABLIS, though they can vary in quality. Wines labelled Mâcon-Villages come from individual villages in the region like **Mâcon-Lugny** or **Mâcon-Viré** are likely to be more rewarding than basic **Mâcon Blanc.** ☆☆

MONTAGNY

 A white wine appellation in the Côte Chalonnaise that tends to offer a more contemporary, fuller style of white burgundy. Other lesser-known appellations that offer good value for money in this part of BURGUNDY are **Mercurey** and **Rully.** ☆☆

PINOT BLANC

 Best examples have traditionally come from the Alsace region of France which offers an elegant and creamy style, not dissimilar from a light CHARDONNAY. Some impressive Pinot Blanc is also produced in Austria and Germany under the name **Weissburgunder.** ☆☆

PINOT GRIS – North America

 The ABC (Anything But Chardonnay) tendency is very taken at the moment with Pinot Gris: a grape that can be fashioned into a smooth stylish peachy-apricotty white, with crisper acidity than its ubiquitous rival. Some very good examples are coming from New Zealand, Oregon, and Canada, and it is popular in the States along with its crisper manifestation Pinot Grigio. ☆☆

ROUSSANNE, MARSANNE, and other Southern French whites

 The quality of whites from the Southern Rhône, the Languedoc, and Roussillon has dramatically improved over the last few years, based on indigenous grape varieties such as Roussanne, Marsanne, and Viognier. They tend to be full and fruity with an attractive apricot character, especially if they include Viognier. Many are simply labelled Côteaux du Langedoc though recognition is expected for individual appellations such as Faugeres. ☆ → ☆☆

ST-VERAN

 This is a village within the MACON appellation in the south of BURGUNDY which generally produces good value wines with an attractively rich, creamy texture. It is often referred to as poor man's **Pouilly-Fuissé** (its more famous neighbouring wine) which spends longer in oak and generally has a fuller style (*see pages 48–53*). ☆☆

SEMILLON

 Although Semillon, like Chardonnay, can be full-bodied in character, inexpensive Semillon, or Semillon/Sauvignon tends to be medium-bodied, though it can have a touch of acidity when young that you could argue puts it into the Crisp Dry White category. Chilean Semillon and Semillon/Sauvignons from Western Australia tend to be lighter in style than Semillons from South Australia (see page 50) with a fresh pineapple and citrus fruit flavour. *See also* Bordeaux Blanc. ☆ → ☆☆

SEMILLON/CHARDONNAY

 "Sém/Chard" as it's jocularly known in the trade is a popular duo that features in a number of Australia's more inexpensive brands. Fruitier than CHARDONNAY on its own, less rich and full-bodied than straight Australian Semillon (*see pages 48–53*), it provides attractively uncomplicated, fruity drinking. Chardonnay lovers may find it a little sweet, but, nevertheless, these wines provide a good starting point for newcomers to wine. ☆→☆☆

SICILY

 Produced much further south than most Italian whites, Sicilian whites have always been rather more full-bodied, but the introduction of modern winemaking techniques by visiting winemakers and inspired use of the local grape varieties like Catarratto, Grecanico, Grillo, and Inzolia have resulted in some really characterful fruity whites. An up-and-coming area that should continue to offer exceptionally good value for money. ☆

SOAVE CLASSICO

 A much-improved region that offers increasingly reliable drinking. Better quality wines, usually labelled "Classico", have an attractive smooth, creamy texture and a delicate almondy flavour. ☆☆

VERDELHO

 A grape, traditionally used for the production of madeira, which has been given a new lease of life, particularly by winemakers in Australia. The resulting wines are juicy and refreshing with an appealing limey fruitiness. ☆☆

VIOGNIER

 Viognier has become much more popular in the last few years and inexpensive examples from the Langedoc and Argentina with their attractive apricot fruit character offer an appealing alternative to Chardonnay. ☆

VIURA

 The Spanish grape that has always been the backbone of white RIOJA is now getting a chance to star on its own. Oaked versions have a pleasingly light, creamy flavour. ☆

Storing and serving

Drink lightly chilled (no longer than an hour in the fridge). Chilling this style of wine too much can dull its delicate flavours. Drink more inexpensive bottles within about three months. A better quality wine like a Chablis or St-Veran will keep much longer, though it may lose something of its initial freshness.

RICH, FULL-BODIED WHITES

A few years ago, when the fashion for big oaky Chardonnays was at its height, you would have found more wines in this section. That was when every winemaker wanted to copy the full-bodied, tropical fruity style that had proved so popular in California and Australia. Now the pendulum has swung back. Just as people are increasingly turning to a lighter style of food, they're looking for lighter, more refreshing wines.

So where does that leave Chardonnay? As mentioned in the previous section, it now has a foot firmly in both camps. Most inexpensive and moderately priced Chardonnays are now made in a lighter, smoother style, while more expensive ones tend to be rich and full-bodied. (Why give customers lashings of expensive oak for nothing if they're equally happy without it?)

The chief characteristics of these fuller Chardonnays – for it is this grape that again dominates this section – are concentration and complexity. This comes partly from the careful selection of vineyards. The New World has discovered what the Old World has known for years, the importance of terroir – the unique configuration of situation, soil and climate that makes one site so much better than another. Increasingly, Californian and Australian wines indicate a more specific area of origin: not just Napa, but Carneros and Sonoma, not southeast Australia, but Padthaway and the Adelaide Hills.

The winemaker's mixing palette

A show-piece Chardonnay may have as many as five or six components including wines from different sites, some unoaked, some barrel-fermented, some fermented in stainless steel but then put into barrels which could be brand new, one or two years old and lightly or more heavily charred. As a result, the winemaker can build up a complex palette of flavours: vanilla oak gives way to cream, mango to apricot, grapefruit, and lime, simple sweetness to refreshing acidity, with oak blending in seamlessly to give an overall richness and a long, lingering finish.

The result is that it's now more difficult to tell top Chardonnays apart. On the whole, those from the New World will be a little sweeter, a little smoother, richer, and more buttery, but they can vary; professional tasters can and do get it wrong. Where they still differ is in their capacity to age. Even the best New World examples age less seductively, developing a rather heavy, slightly cloying character, instead of the rich nuttiness and thrilling acidity of the best white burgundy. You'd drink most top Californian or Australian Chardonnay within three to five years. A Montrachet or Corton-Charlemagne could easily survive twenty.

Longevity is also a feature of the other top wines of this section. Wines like Hermitage and the classed-growths of Bordeaux such as those of Pessac-Léognan/Graves create extraordinarily opulent, complex wines which, in the best vintages, will last several decades.

More affordable versions of both, albeit of a different character, can be found in Australia. The Marsanne grape, on which Hermitage is based, and Semillon, the basis of white Bordeaux (with Sauvignon Blanc), both star on their own Down Under. When young they taste like any other fruity Australian white, but after a few years both develop the most marvellous roast pineapple and dried fruit flavours.

To sum up, these are generally not the kind of wines you'd drink routinely. Most are too expensive, or too rich for everyday drinking. Save them for special occasions and for people you know are going to enjoy the experience as much as you will: the kind of meal where the wine comes first, then you wonder what you're going to eat with it.

Label clues

Most of these wines will be high in alcohol: 13.5–14.5 degrees. Check the vintage. A wine older than three years may not be as fresh and fruity as you're used to, but it may be more complex. Look at the back label to see how long the wine has spent in oak: more than twelve months and it is likely to have a more pronounced, oaky character.

Above Rich, buttery California Chardonnays from wineries such as the picturesque Fetzer (above) provide reliably full-bodied drinking.

Far left The Hunter Valley in Australia is producing slightly more subtle styles of Chardonnay than were previously popular. The wines are big, but with a little less oak and more complexity of flavour.

Starting points	
European style Chardonnay	**Anything but Chardonnay**
Fine white burgundy Cool climate California Chardonnay	Barossa Semillon Australian Marsanne Traditional white Rioja Pessac-Léognan (Graves)
New World Chardonnay	
South African Chardonnay Australian Chardonnay New Zealand Chardonnay	

BAROSSA VALLEY and other South Australian Semillon

Australian Semillon confusingly comes in several styles from the almost Riesling-like Semillons of the Hunter Valley to the elegant Sauvignon/Semillon blends of Western Australia. But those from the Barossa Valley and other hotter parts of South Australia have a particularly rich, lush, full-bodied, fresh pineapple fruit that make them a great choice for lovers of full-bodied whites. ☆☆

BURGUNDY

There is no white wine as opulently sensual as an expensive white burgundy, the finest expression of the CHARDONNAY grape. The extraordinary interplay of flavours – butter, cream, hazelnuts, peach, lime, the odd hint of cinnamon spice – make it a once-tried-never-forgotten experience. This complexity takes time to evolve. Few wines of this class are ready to drink before they are three years old and they may continue to improve until they are eight or ten. The effect of age changes the wines' character, making them less creamy, softer, richer, and more honeyed, with even a slightly oily or savoury character that you may or may not like.

Burgundy's vineyards can be difficult to get a grip on because of the multiplicity of different names. Most growing areas have wines that are labelled *premier cru* or *grand cru* which come from specific parcels of land which were singled out during the last century as producing wines of the highest quality. *grand cru* (theoretically at least) signifies the finest wines, *premier cru* the next best, but the very finest examples undoubtedly come from tiny production areas such as CORTON-CHARLEMAGNE.

Unfortunately, not all burgundy hits these giddy heights, so it pays to buy from a specialist merchant or a sommelier who knows his wine list well. Be suspicious of wines of this reputation that are offered at well below the normal price.

Lesser-known white burgundies in this style which can offer particularly good value for money are **Auxey-Duresses**, **Pernand-Vergelesses**, **St-Aubin,** and **St-Romain**. These villages are well worth looking out for. ☆☆☆

CHABLIS GRAND CRU

Although basic Chablis is dry and flinty, the top-quality wines which are labelled *grand cru* fall firmly in this category. They include Blanchot, Bougros, Les Clos, Grenouilles, Les Preuses, Valmur, and Vaudésir. Some *premier cru* wines could be classified as full-bodied, though there are now so many of them (they account for about a quarter of the region's wines) that many are frankly not a lot better than basic Chablis.

Given some bottle age, Chablis develops powerful, rich, almost tropical flavours – quite different from the lean, steely quality of its youth. *Grand cru* Chablis shouldn't be drunk for at least five years and can age magnificently for ten years or even longer. ☆☆☆

CHARDONNAY – oak-aged

Europe (excluding France) Most inexpensive oak-aged European Chardonnays are made in a lighter style than this, an exception being

those from Sicily and Spanish regions such as Navarra and Somontano which are producing some impressively toasty full-bodied Chardonnays at a very reasonable price. Top producers all over Europe including Austria, Greece, Italy, and Spain also include world class Chardonnays in their repertoire, two examples being Jermann's "Dreams" and Torres' "Milmanda". ☆→☆☆☆

California There may have been a reaction against Chardonnay among the cognoscenti (witness the Anything But Chardonnay movement), but most North American wine-drinkers, and winemakers, still take the variety very seriously. Nowhere is that more the case than in California, which makes some of the highest quality white wines outside Burgundy in areas such as the Napa, Alexander, and Russian River Valleys. Some superb Chardonnay is also produced to the south of San Francisco in Monterey County, and in the Edna and Santa Maria Valleys of the Central Coast. ☆☆→☆☆☆

Canada This country has advanced by leaps and bounds as a Chardonnay producer in recent years and now turns out some weightily impressive wines. Most of these come from the Ontario region. ☆☆→☆☆☆

New York State Just over the border from Ontario, the wines of New York State are very similar in character. Some quite CHABLIS-like examples come from producers in Long Island and around the Finger Lakes. ☆☆→☆☆☆

Pacific Northwest (Oregon and Washington State) So far Washington has the edge over Oregon as a Chardonnay producer, creating richly fruity full-bodied Chardonnays in a typically Californian style. Oregon's wines could turn out in the longer term to be a closer approximation to BURGUNDY'S, particularly as some of the smaller producers adopt more traditional methods. ☆☆→☆☆☆

Australia Just as everybody thought they knew where they were with Australian Chardonnay, the goal posts have moved. The big walloping oaky style of the late 1980s and early 1990s has fallen out of fashion, in favour of much more restrained wines: not burgundy certainly, but Chardonnay that often shows a creamily elegant character and a much fresher acidity than in the past. The most prized vineyards are now those in cooler areas: the Clare and Eden Valleys, Padthaway, and the Adelaide Hills in South Australia and the Yarra Valley in Victoria. Even in the hot, humid Hunter Valley there is a new region called Orange that has proved particularly promising for Chardonnay. Wines that are made in Western Australia, too, are far removed from the stereotype. Chardonnays from such top producers as Cullen, Leeuwin, and Piero can hold their own with the world's best. Make no mistake, these are still big wines, but they are altogether more serious than the simple, uncomplicated fruit-and-oak recipe Chardonnays we were used to. ☆☆→☆☆☆

New Zealand It's ironic that New Zealand is best-known for its Sauvignon when its Chardonnay is so fine. The economics of the industry here mean that very few inexpensive wines are produced, which justifies generous expenditure on good quality oak barrels. There are detectable regional differences: Chardonnays from the Gisborne and Hawkes Bay areas on the North Island show a more obviously tropical fruit character than those from the cooler Marlborough region of the South Island. As with Australia though, there are significant differences within regions too. The Wairarapa area to the south of the North Island, for example, produces a classically creamy Burgundian style of Chardonnay. Overall though, expect big, full-bodied wines with a noticeable oak influence, in a style that falls somewhere between those of Australia and California. ☆☆→☆☆☆

South Africa Although most inexpensive Chardonnays fall within the previous style section, South Africa is also one of the cheapest producers of a more full-bodied style. There is also an increasing number of more expensive Chardonnays being produced by such producers as De Wetshof and Vergelegen which, while they have yet to reach the standard of the best the New World has to offer, are certainly within sight of it. ☆☆

Chile Only Chile's top ranking reserva Chardonnays are full-bodied enough to fall into this section, but they too are on the increase. Like so many of Chile's wines, they offer good value for money. ☆☆

Argentina This country is now approximately where Chile was about five years ago with regard to white winemaking. Chardonnays therefore tend to be more obviously oaky, but most have the virtue of being extremely good value. ☆→☆☆

Food and occasions

These more full-bodied whites can be partnered by equally richly flavoured food. Save fine whites from Bordeaux and Burgundy and the best New World Chardonnays for special occasions, and lavish ingredients like turbot and lobster. More inexpensive wines like Australian Chardonnays and Semillons go well with a modern European or slightly spicy Asian-influenced style of cooking.

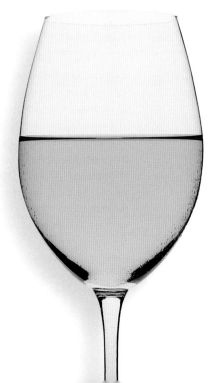

CORTON-CHARLEMAGNE

Fabulously lush creamy, buttery *grand cru* from the village of Aloxe-Corton to the north of the COTE DE BEAUNE that can take several years to reveal its true magnificence. Very scarce and very expensive. ☆☆☆

HERMITAGE and other top whites from the Rhône

One of the greatest white wines of the Rhône with a formidable reputation for longevity, Hermitage is based on the classic southern French grape varieties of Marsanne and Roussanne. White Châteauneuf-du-Pape, based on the same varieties, comes into a similar category – rich, full, and spicy. Although producers have responded to the public's desire for more immediate gratification, both are more complex and rewarding after a few years' ageing. ☆☆☆

JURANCON SEC

An obscure but delightful curiosity, this elegant, dry, spicy, full-bodied wine is made in the southwest of France near the Pyrenees. It also has a delicious sweet counterpart (*see* pages 92–7). ☆☆→☆☆☆

MARSANNE

This grape variety is the unsung hero of white wines from the RHONE but its main claim to fame is the varietal wines it makes in a very specific area of Australia: Victoria's Goulbourn Valley. There two producers, Chateau Tahbilk

and Mitchelton make some remarkably deep-coloured wines with rich baked pineapple and grilled grapefruit flavours which, like SEMILLON, are at their most rewarding after several years' ageing. It also makes some impressive wines in California. ☆☆

MEURSAULT

The largest wine commune of the fabled COTE DE BEAUNE producing big, full-bodied CHARDONNAYS with a rich butterscotch, toasty oak character. Although there are no *grands crus* in this commune, most wines are full-bodied. One of the more widely available of the top white burgundies and a reasonably reliable buy on wine lists. ☆☆☆

PESSAC-LEOGNAN (GRAVES)

The most prestigious area for dry white wine production in Bordeaux, formerly part of the Graves appellation. This is SEMILLON and SAUVIGNON at their finest: graceful, elegant, creamy, with the capacity to age for many years – even decades – and an ideal refuge for wine enthusiasts looking for alternatives to CHARDONNAY. ☆☆→☆☆☆

POUILLY-FUISSE

The most famous of the white wines from the Mâconnais, the south of the Burgundy region. There are no *premier* or *grand cru* wines: the best come from single vineyards and consistently reliable producers such as Ferret, Guffens-Heynen, and Marcel Vincent at Château Fuissé. ☆☆→☆☆☆

PULIGNY-MONTRACHET & CHASSAGNE- MONTRACHET

Two villages to the south of the COTE DE BEAUNE which at their best produce some of the most seductively elegant and creamy of all white BURGUNDIES. The finest of all come from individual *grand cru* vineyards like **Le Montrachet** and **Bâtard-Montrachet** which span the two growing areas. But the very limited size of these (Bâtard-Montrachet has twelve hectares, Le Montrachet eight, and **Bienvenues-Bâtard-Montrachet** only four) ensures that these wines remain the province of millionaire wine collectors. Puligny- and Chassagne-Montrachet are more affordable but still by no means cheap. ☆☆→☆☆☆

RIOJA – traditional whites

Although the fashion in Rioja now is for much fresher whites, you can still find examples of wines made in a more traditional style from bodegas such as Lopez de Heredia and Muga. Aged for up to four years in big oak casks, they acquire a slightly baked, oxidized flavour that is at odds with many modern wine drinkers' tastes, though they are much appreciated by wine enthusiasts looking for wines with real individuality. Wines labelled "*crianza*" (which are aged for a minimum of six months) are likely to be lighter than those labelled "*reserva*" or "*gran reserva*" which have to be aged for two and four years respectively. ☆☆

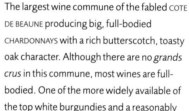

SAUVIGNON BLANC

While most Sauvignon tastes light, fresh, and crisp, the top wines from producers in the Loire, New Zealand, Styria in Austria, and the Constantia region of South Africa have an intensity that can aptly be described as full-bodied. That can depend on any one or a combination of factors – exceptionally ripe grapes, oak-ageing, lees stirring (*see* page 28) or a proportion of Semillon being included in the blend. ☆☆→☆☆☆

SEMILLON

See Barossa Semillon.

VIOGNIER – Californian and Australian

At its most intense Viognier might be regarded as an aromatic wine, but the levels of alcohol which can easily reach 14.5per cent ABV in hot climates such as Australia and California also place it in the full-bodied category. It has a rich, almost waxy texture and a distinctive, lush apricot flavour that are recognizable when even quite a small amount is included in a blend. ☆☆

VIN JAUNE

A totally distinctive style of wine made in a very similar way to fino sherry. The most famous example is from the tiny appellation of **Château-Chalon** in the Jura region in France. ☆☆☆

Storing and serving

Wines like this repay the same care as the winemaker puts into them. Don't chill them too much before you serve them and don't be afraid to open them an hour or so before you pour them into a generously sized wine glass to reveal their complex flavours. Inexpensive oaky Chardonnnays will last for a couple of years. Most New World Chardonnay is at its best from three to five years old, top white burgundy from five to eight years, and the very best white wines for up to fifteen to twenty years. Australian Semillons and Marsannes are also long-lived. They'll be fine for four to eight years.

AROMATIC AND MEDIUM-DRY WHITES

Of all the different wine styles this is by far the most eclectic, covering an extraordinary number of widely differing flavours. None of them is exactly a mainstream taste – though there are wines that have a fanatical following. Chardonnay never quite excites a Chardonnay lover the way a fine Riesling excites a Riesling devotee.

The common thread which distinguishes them from other white wines is some kind of aromatic or floral quality which makes them taste not sweet, but not quite dry either. In most cases this sweetness is offset by a crisp acidity so that the overall effect is deliciously refreshing.

Germany has most to offer in this style, but, unfortunately, has the distinction of producing some of the least exciting wine in the world as well as some of the best. Sadly, many consumers whose wine-drinking experience starts with German wine never get beyond the dreariest bottles, then abandon them as unsophisticated when their wine tastes change. Alsace, another great producer of aromatic wines, and with traditionally close links to Germany, gets tarred with the same brush.

The flavour of most of the wines in this section comes from the grapes themselves. Whereas the taste of a Chardonnay often owes as much to the type of oak it is aged in as to the fruit, wines like Riesling and Gewurztraminer are made without going near a new oak barrel. Traditional producers still use big oak casks, but most are so old that they impart very little flavour of their own. The emphasis is on the vineyard rather than the winery – a question of obtaining the best possible fruit from the best possible sites, then letting it speak for itself.

Dry or sweet?

The big variation between, say, one Riesling and another, is in the level of sweetness. That depends on the grapes' ripeness when picked and how dry or sweet the winemaker intends the wine to be (see pages 26–31).

All these variations are reflected in a multiplicity of classifications. In Germany better quality dry wines are labelled "Kabinett", "Spätlese" or "Auslese", but "Auslese" and occasionally "Spätlese" can also be quite sweet. The same is true of "Vendange Tardive" (late-picked) in Alsace. It isn't always easy to see what is going on in a bottle, even from the label; so don't be afraid to ask just how dry or sweet a wine is. It doesn't indicate a lack of know-how – quite the reverse!

The other common characteristic of many of these wines is just how long they can age; some of the top Rieslings and some of the Loire's best Chenin Blanc-based wines such as Vouvray and

Savennières will last for decades. This is not a characteristic that appeals to everyone. Riesling, for example, acquires over time a distinctive kerosene flavour that is a far cry from the clean fruit flavours of most modern varietals.

It may be for this reason that the more aromatic grapes have not always found favour with consumers who are used to more upfront fruit flavours. But, with the increasing popularity of Asian-influenced food and the constant demand for new experiences among more adventurous wine-drinkers, the situation has been changing. Australia has led the way with its distructive, rich, limey Riesling and there are attractive Gewurztraminers from elsewhere in the New World, such as New Zealand, Chile, Oregon, and New York State.

In fact, it is the image much more than the reality of many of these wines that holds people back. When they taste them, they like them – and even more so when they find out how low in alcohol they are. For today's adventurous health-conscious wine-drinker this light but beguilingly flavoursome style of wine has a great deal to recommend it.

Label clues

It can be difficult to tell how sweet this type of wine is but "Spätlese", "Auslese" or "Vendange Tardive" generally indicate a more concentrated wine. Look out, too, for the words "*demi-sec*" and "*halbtrocken*" which mean medium-dry. And check the vintage: older wines are more likely to have those pungent lime and kerosene flavours.

Above *The picturesque village of Hunawihr in Alsace is surrounded by some of the region's finest vineyards.*

Far left *The spectacular steep banks of the River Mosel in Germany provide ideal conditions for ripening the Riesling grape. The vineyards are angled towards the sun which is reflected back up to the vines by the water.*

Starting points	
Light/floral	**Rich/aromatic**
Sylvaner	Australian Riesling
Riesling Kabinett	Riesling Spätlese
	Tokay-Pinot Gris
Fragrant/spicy	**Medium-dry**
Torrontes	Vouvray
Dry Muscat	New World Colombard
Viognier	
Gewurztraminer	

ANJOU & SAUMUR BLANC – demi-sec

Medium-dry versions of Anjou Blanc and Saumur Blanc from the Loire region of France are sold alongside their dry counterparts, but are rarely particularly exciting. ☆→☆☆

AUSTRALIAN "DRY WHITES"

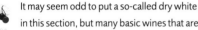

It may seem odd to put a so-called dry white in this section, but many basic wines that are labelled "Dry White" are not strictly dry at all. This is particularly true of wines from New World countries such as Australia, New Zealand, Chile, and Argentina which contain enough of an aromatic grape like MULLER-THURGAU, MUSCAT or TORRONTES to give them a slightly floral character. (Check the back label for words such as "fragrant" or "aromatic".) ☆→☆☆

CHENIN BLANC – mature, dry

Like RIESLING, the top Chenin Blancs of the Loire develop a distinctive aromatic character after several years in the bottle, becoming richly honeyed, with an almost nutty savouriness. Only the best wines like dry **Vouvrays** and **Savennières** are worth keeping this long – and there isn't much of them about. ☆☆→☆☆☆

COLOMBARD

Although generally regarded as a dry white wine, Colombard is often made by Australian and South African winemakers in a slightly sweetish style which makes it a good choice for those looking for an off-dry white. CHARDONNAY that is blended with Colombard will also tend to be left with comparatively high levels of residual sugar. ☆

CONDRIEU

Expensive and highly sought-after, this northern Rhône white wine is VIOGNIER at its most exotically perfumed best. Even rarer (and more stratospheric in price) are the wines from the tiny neighbouring appellation **Château-Grillet**. ☆☆☆

FURMINT

Best-known for the part it plays in Hungary's great sweet wine Tokaj (see pages 92–7), this grape is also used to make spicy, slightly earthy whites which are drier and more full-bodied than most aromatic wines. ☆→☆☆

GEWURZTRAMINER

The tasting terms that are commonly used of Gewürztraminer – rose petals, lychees, and Turkish delight – underline its status as the world's most exotic-flavoured white wine grape. It is still a wine that is primarily associated with Alsace in France where it is at its richly spicy best, but it has also attracted a fair amount of attention from New World producers. Inexpensive versions from South Africa, Chile, and California tend to be fresher and more floral. Those from New Zealand, Canada, and Oregon are more complex. ☆→☆☆☆

GRUNER VELTLINER – mature

Top quality Grüner Veltliner, which is grown mainly in the Wachau region of Austria, ages very much like the best RIESLING Spätlese, developing powerful aromatic spicy flavours. The best-quality wines are classified as *smaragd* and must have an alcohol content of more than twelve per cent. ☆☆→☆☆☆

HARSLEVELU

Hungarian grape used either on its own or as a named component of blends with other indigenous grapes such as FURMINT to make inexpensive, crisp, aromatic whites. ☆

IRSAI OLIVER

An aromatic grape variety (also spelt Irsay Oliver) mainly planted in Hungary, Slovenia, and the Czech Republic. It has a slightly MUSCAT-like flavour. ☆

LAMBRUSCO

Pallid, sweetish, slightly fizzy Italian white from Emilia-Romagna that does little justice to the original crisp, lively red wines of the same name that come from the region. Much less popular than it once was. ☆

LASKI RIESLING

The name used in Slovenia for the Welschriesling grape, largely used to make dull, oversweetened whites that acquired considerable popularity during the heyday of LIEBFRAUMILCH under the brandname Lutomer Riesling. In fact, the grape can produce some deliciously fresh, aromatic whites, but they are rarely available outside the country. ☆

LIEBFRAUMILCH and other medium-dry German whites

Cheap German semi-sweet wines such as Liebfraumilch, **Hock**, **Piesporter Michelsberg,** and **Niersteiner** used to account for a large proportion of the market. But now they are increasingly (and justifiably) being eclipsed by better quality wines that offer more than simple sweetness. ☆

MARLBOROUGH SAUVIGNON BLANC

So intense are the gooseberry and asparagus flavours of Sauvignon Blanc produced in the Marlborough region of New Zealand that many people would consider them aromatic. Winemakers in other countries and in cooler vintages may also produce Sauvignons in this style but none do so quite as consistently as those in New Zealand. ☆☆→☆☆☆

MULLER-THURGAU

A cross between RIESLING and SYLVANER, Müller-Thurgau has been the undistinguished mainstay of LIEBFRAUMILCH and many of Germany's cheaper whites. It is also used by English producers of medium-dry styles. But some of the crisp, clean, and fruity bottles emerging from New Zealand show that the grape has more potential than has been realised up to now. ☆→☆☆

MUSCAT – dry

Whether you regard dry Muscat as dry or not depends on your palate. Most of course is very sweet – only suitable for drinking with a dessert – but there are drier versions, particularly in Alsace and down in the Languedoc in the south of France which the locals would drink as an apéritif. The Alsace version is particularly fine – light, elegant grapey, and refreshing. A small proportion of Muscat is often used by a winemaker in a blend to give his wine a more pronounced floral or aromatic character. Dry Muscats are also popular in Hungary and can offer good value for money. ☆→☆☆

RETSINA

A controversial style of Greek wine which has the distinctive aroma and flavour of pine needles (some rudely say disinfectant) which actually comes from infusing lumps of resin in the fermenting wine. It comes in both white and rosé versions and should be well-chilled. ☆

Food and occasions

These idiosyncratic wines are not to everyone's taste so it's a case of knowing your guest. Most work better as an aperitif rather than a wine to take you through the meal, though though they come into their own with spicy cuisines such as Thai, Vietnamese, Chinese, and milder Indian dishes. Gewürztraminer and Tokay-Pinot Gris can be a good non-sweet option with foie gras.

RIESLING

Germany Riesling has suffered badly from being confused with inexpensive German wines like Liebfraumilch which are made from entirely different grapes. But genuine Riesling's unique balance of refreshingly crisp acidity and delicate sweetness makes it taste like no other wine on earth.

How then do you tell the good from the bad? The best guide is the classification system for higher quality (QmP) wines: they are labelled according to their level of ripeness. The three grades that apply to dry (as opposed to dessert wines) are Kabinett, Spätlese, and Auslese. Kabinett wines are light and crisp, Spätlese (literally, late-picked) fuller and more rounded, and Auslese (which is made from very ripe grapes and normally made into a sweeter style of wine) richer still. Winemakers also use the word "*trocken*" or "*halbtrocken*" (medium-dry) to indicate that their wine is made in a drier style.

There are also differences in style between one growing area and another. The Mosel-Saar-Ruwer produces Riesling at its most rarefied and racy, very low in alcohol and deliciously light. The wines from the Rheingau, and the Pfalz are richer and more full-bodied with a lush almost peachy character. The Nahe and the Rheinhessen are more varied in quality with the best of the wines from the Nahe leaning towards the style of the Mosel and those of the Rheinhessen (which is still an area that produces huge quantities of low grade wine) being more similar to those of the Rheingau and Pfalz.

The other big dividing line is between young and mature Riesling. Young Riesling, particularly that from the Mosel, can taste toothacheingly sharp, but give it a few years and it develops a gloriously lush limey, almost petrolly character (which is a great deal nicer than it sounds). Others acquire a softer, richer more honeyed flavour. The best will continue to improve for several years. ☆☆→☆☆☆

Alsace These Rieslings are bigger and more alcoholic than Germany's with richer fruit flavours and a touch of spice, though again, like Germany, there are variations in sweetness. The most sumptuous are those from the top *grand cru* vineyards. ☆☆→☆☆☆

Australia A good starting point for first time Riesling drinkers, Australia's Rieslings share the same full-bodied fruity character as its other wines. The best come from the Clare and Eden Valleys in South Australia where they develop a marvellously tangy limey character. ☆☆→☆☆☆

Austria Some of Austria's finest wines are made from the Riesling grape; notably in the Wachau and Kremstal regions of the country. Although they have similar classifications to German Rieslings they are more similar in style to those from Alsace with a higher alcohol content than is typical in northern Germany. ☆☆→☆☆☆

New Zealand With a cooler climate than Australia, New Zealand Riesling is lighter and more elegant than its Antipodean counterpart, with more of the ripe peachy notes and kerosene character you get in the warmer growing areas of Germany. ☆☆→☆☆☆

North America Until recently Riesling was not really rated in the USA. In California and the Pacific Northwest, where it is known as Johannisberg Riesling, it was traditionally used to make straightforward, light, citrussy, off-dry whites for everyday drinking. But producers in Oregon, Ontario, and New York State are now producing fine examples in the classic European style. ☆☆→☆☆☆

SCHEUREBE

A comparatively new grape variety (a cross between RIESLING and SYLVANER) which has found favour with a number of Germany's top winemakers, particularly in the Pfalz. It can produce lovely lush, spicy whites with a seductive interplay of grapefruit and exotic fruits. ☆☆→☆☆☆

SEYVAL BLANC

A relatively undistinguished French hybrid grape which is popular in England and other cooler regions including Canada and New York State for making crisp, floral, as well as medium-dry whites. ☆→☆☆

SYLVANER

The lightest style of the wines from Alsace, Sylvaner produces a fresh, slightly floral wine that is markedly drier than German white in a similar price bracket. It is also one of the grapes used to make a light, fruity white called Edelzwicker – rarely found outside Alsace, but a simple, refreshing wine to drink when you are visiting the region. (The German name for the grape is Silvaner.) ☆→☆☆

TOKAJ-PINOT GRIS

Confusingly, Pinot Gris is often called Tokaj-Pinot Gris in Alsace, but should not be confused with Hungarian Tokaj, which is an entirely different, sweeter wine (*see* pages 92–7.) Alsace Pinot Gris is a much richer style than that grown elsewhere and the best examples have an exotic musky character. Vendange Tardive versions can be comparatively sweet (*see also* pages 92–7). ☆☆→☆☆☆

TORRONTES

Originally a Spanish grape variety, Torrontes has become a popular variety in Argentina. It produces light, floral, intensely perfumed whites which make for charmingly easy drinking when young, but which fade very quickly after a year or so. Be sure to drink the current vintage. ☆

VIOGNIER

The powerfully high alcohol levels of Viogniers from hot climates such as those in California and Austria have made "full-bodied" a more accurate classification (*see* page 53) but there are still Viogniers, notably from France (*see* CONDRIEU) where the aromatic quality is the most noticeable characteristic. Price tends to be the determining factor. Inexpensive Viogniers taste more like Chardonnay (see p47) while more expensive bottles will display more exotic fruit (apricot) and a spicy, musky character. Like Muscat, a small amount in a blend can have a disproportionate influence. ☆☆→☆☆☆

VOUVRAY – demi-sec

The most highly regarded medium-dry white is demi-sec Vouvray which comes from the Loire region of France. While some can be as dull as other less distinguished medium-dry Loire whites, the best wines from individual producers such as Brédif and Huët have a deliciously rich, smooth honeyed flavour. A similar style is available from the **Montlouis** appellation, the other side of Loire. Make sure you look carefully at the label. Both are also made in dry (*sec*) and sweet (*moelleux*) versions. ☆☆→☆☆☆

WHITE ZINFANDEL

Confusingly the hugely popular White Zinfandel is not really a white wine at all as it is made from the red Zinfandel grape. The same applies to **White Grenache** and **White Merlot**. (*See* Rosé section pages 82–5.) ☆

Storing and serving

This type of wine benefits from being well chilled. While some varieties such as Sylvaner, Torrontes, and Viognier should be drunk soon after you buy them, others like Chenin Blanc, Grüner Veltliner, Riesling, and Tokaj-Pinot Gris can last for many years. By and large it is the wines with the most marked levels of acidity that have the greatest staying power.

LIGHT, FRUITY REDS

People are attracted to lighter red wines for a variety of reasons. Firstly it's a good starting point for the new red wine drinker, not only from the point of view of their palate (these wines are neither tough or tannic), but their pocket. Almost all inexpensive reds come into this category, whether it's a *vin rouge*, *vino rosso* or *vino tinto*. They're the kind of wines you find served by the carafe at a French café or an Italian *trattoria*.

By contrast, this style also appeals to experienced wine-drinkers who gear their wine choice to the occasion and the time of year. For them, lesser-known Loire reds or a delicate Pinot Noir make perfect summer drinking or less conventional choice with fish.

Finally, there are people who discover this style and stick with it. Those who prefer their red wine soft and fruity, rather than full-bodied and oaky, who enjoy the sheer refreshing gulpability of a Valpolicella and a Beaujolais. Truly this style has something for everyone.

Most wines are light because they are designed to be so, usually because the producer has to make them to a price. The traditional way, much favoured by small wine-growers all over Europe, was to allow your vines to produce as prolifically as possible and to do as little as you could get away with to the resulting wine. The result was often dull and dilute.

Hi-tech winemaking

When quality is at a premium, wines owe their style far more to what goes on in the winery. Producing a light red wine involves sophisticated techniques like carbonic maceration and cold soaking (*see* pages 26–31) to preserve its bright fruit flavours, fermenting it at cool temperatures in stainless steel, and avoiding the use of expensive oak barrels which push up the price and make the wine more full-bodied.

This is why grapes like Grenache and Tempranillo, better-known for big-tasting wines, are in this section. The difference is in the degree of concentration. Where a winemaker uses grapes from younger vines, or less favoured vineyards the wine will be lighter – as low as eleven per cent.

Climate also has a part to play in how a red wine tastes. On the whole this is not a style of wine you generally find in the New World. In hotter climates grapes ripen more fully and that sweetness converts to higher levels of alcohol. The only New World wines you'll consistently find in this style are basic reds like a "Cape red", "Chilean red" or "Argentinian red" which are made to a price and to satisfy the maximum number of different palates. A good vintage will also make a difference, particularly in Europe. If you regularly taste Beaujolais Nouveau when it comes out, for example, you'll notice that some years it tastes much riper and fruitier than others. A simple Côtes du Rhône, too, will taste much richer and fuller in a year like 2003 than a poor year like 2002.

There are also grapes which are naturally light and fruity and particularly attractive unoaked. This is true of both Gamay and Pinot Noir and also of the lesser-known Italian grapes that make such wines as Valpolicella. Keeping them away from oak is not only a question of keeping the cost down, but of preserving the pure flavour of the fruit. With more expensive reds such as those from the Loire, producers may age their wines in oak, but the long ripening period in that cool region gives the wines an intensity of fruit that offsets any overt oakiness.

The major variations within this style are between sharpness and smoothness. Some wines, particularly the lighter Italian wines, like Bardolino or Valpolicella, and Beaujolais, have naturally tart fruit. This can be disguised by adding sugar (chaptalization); but better winemakers won't do this. They can be tremendously refreshing when chilled during the summer, but some wine-drinkers can find them uncomfortably sharp and acidic. Other grape varieties like Merlot, Pinot Noir and Dornfelder are much softer and smoother and therefore much more approachable.

What most of these wines have in common is that they offer simple, straightforward drinking. Buy them, take them home, and drink them within a week, if not the same night – these are not wines to store or worry about cellaring. There is a place for them in everyone's collection.

Label clues

The two best indications of a lighter style of wine are alcohol content and vintage. Red wines under 12.5 degrees will almost always be light and fruity. Look out for the most recent vintage – wines that are two or three years old may start to taste dull and flabby rather than vibrantly fruity.

Above *Valpolicella in northeast Italy is the source of a large range of fruity red wines. The picture shows part of the "Classico" zone which offers better quality.*

Far left *The beautiful region of Beaujolais in France produces distinctively juicy, cherry-flavoured red wines.*

Starting points	
Fresh, fruity	**Soft, smooth**
Beaujolais	Inexpensive Merlot
Basic burgundy	Basic Australian/Chilean reds
Côtes du Rhône	Chilean Pinot Noir
Valpolicella	

BARBERA

Traditionally a light red with vibrant berry flavours from the Piedmont region of Italy, most commonly available as Barbera d'Alba and Barbera d'Asti. More expensive examples and those from California, Australia, and Argentina tend to be more full-bodied. ☆

BARDOLINO

An appealing light, fresh, fruity red from the Veneto in the northeast of Italy. Similar in style to Beajolais (*see* below). ☆→☆☆

BEAUJOLAIS

The epitome of light fruity drinking. Made from the GAMAY grape to the south of BURGUNDY, at one stage Beaujolais's youthful cherry-flavoured style was almost unique, but competition from more reliably fruity New World wines has caused its popularity to wane. Most people's first encounter with Beaujolais is **Beaujolais Nouveau**, the first wine of the vintage, released in November within a few weeks of the harvest. Except in a particularly good year it tends to be very light, with a slightly confected flavour irreverently compared to bananas and bubblegum. Basic Beaujolais is often little different although wines from individual producers can be much more impressive. **Beaujolais Villages**, which comes from individual villages in the region, is in theory better still (but that isn't invariably the case). Far more serious are the top ranking so-called "*cru*" Beaujolais though these fall in the next section. ☆→☆☆

BLAUER ZWEIGELT

Also known as Zweigelt, this is a popular Austrian grape variety making smooth, soft plummy reds, often at a modest price. ☆→☆☆

BLAUFRANKISCH/KEKFRANKOS

Another indigenous Austrian grape. Unoaked it makes attractively tart berry-flavoured reds (the style usually made in Hungary where it is called Kékfrankos), but which have a nice spicy kick to them. When oaked it is richer and more full-bodied. ☆☆→☆☆☆

BURGUNDY – inexpensive, unoaked

Because it is generally so expensive, burgundy has the image of being a heavyweight wine. But, in fact, PINOT NOIR – the grape from which it is made – is a naturally light, fragrant variety which, when left unoaked, produces wines with a pure, intense raspberry flavour and deliciously soft, supple texture.

Most basic burgundy is simply labelled "**Bourgogne Rouge**", though producers now occasionally add the words "Pinot Noir". As in neighbouring BEAUJOLAIS, quality varies but the overall standard has improved considerably in recent years. Wines made by individual growers – often just down the road from some of the region's greatest vineyards – can be very fine indeed. **Bourgogne Passe-Tout-Grains** is confusingly not really true burgundy at all, but a blend of Pinot Noir and GAMAY. As you might expect from the grape varieties, it falls somewhere in style between a burgundy and Beaujolais.

Some burgundies from individual villages could also be classed as light and fruity – the most likely candidates are **Chorey-lès-Beaune**, **Marsannay**, **Monthélie**, **Rully**, and occasionally **St-Aubin**. ☆☆

CABERNET FRANC – Old World

The third element of the classic Bordeaux blend, Cabernet Franc is also used in other European wine regions, such as the LOIRE, Eastern Europe, and northern Italy, to make wine on its own. Suited to cooler climates, it is capable of producing quite richly flavoured wines, but with a dryness and slight stalkiness about them that makes them taste comparatively light. Italian versions, mostly from the Friuli region in the northeast, are particularly fruity. ☆☆→☆☆☆

CINSAULT

Cinsault (also spelt Cinsaut) is widely planted in South Africa where it is used in many of its inexpensive reds – sometimes anonymously as a "**Cape Red**", sometimes in a blend with another varietal such as Pinotage, Ruby Cabernet, and even Zinfandel. It has a fairly sweet, jammy taste, though cheaper versions can develop a less appealing, rather rubbery flavour. ☆→☆☆

CORSICA

Increasingly fashionable in France, Corsican reds are generally based on similar varieties to the South of France, as well as indigenous grape varieties Nielluccio and Sciacarello which

tend to produce light cherry flavoured reds.
☆☆

COTES DU RHONE and other basic Southern French reds

Like BEAUJOLAIS, Côtes du Rhône varies considerably in quality from one producer to another and between vintages. In a warm year like 2003, or from a top Rhône producer like Guigal, it can taste sumptuously rich and alcoholic; in a poor vintage or from a less quality conscious co-op, it can be pretty weedy. However, standards have improved and more and more wines are soft and appealing, with an attractive sweet strawberry flavour – offering the typical warmth of a southern French red without the weight that often goes with it. Similar basic reds from other Southern French appellations such as Côtes du Ventoux, Costières de Nîmes, and Côtes du Roussillon can also provide refreshing everyday drinking. ☆→☆☆

DAO and young, Portuguese reds

Portuguese reds invariably used to be heavy and oaky. Not any more. Even wines like Dão are made in a much more upfront fruity style these days. The majority of these lighter, fruitier reds come from the up and coming areas in the centre and south of the country: the Alentejo, Estremadura, and Ribatejo, and can offer very attractive drinking. ☆→☆☆

DOLCETTO

This grape is grown in Piedmont in northwest Italy but makes a very different style of wine to BARBERA, characterized by its intensely vivid brambly fruit (Dolcetto means "little sweet one"). For an Italian wine it has comparatively low acidity. ☆☆

DOLE

Switzerland's most distinctive red, which comes from the Valais region in the French speaking part of the country, is a softly fruity but elegant wine. It is made predominantly from PINOT NOIR blended with a varying amount of GAMAY. ☆☆→☆☆☆

DORNFELDER – unoaked

An indigenous German grape variety which makes the country's best-known home-grown red. Young, unoaked versions which are smooth and softly plummy make particularly easy, approachable drinking for first-time red wine drinkers. Oaked versions are more full-bodied and substantial. ☆→☆☆

GAMAY

Although gamay is identified with BEAUJOLAIS, it is also grown elsewhere in France, mainly in BURGUNDY and the LOIRE. (**Gamay de Touraine** can be better value than basic Beaujolais.)
In Burgundy and Switzerland it is often blended with PINOT NOIR – both red Mâcon and **Bourgogne Passe-Tout-Grains** are blends. ☆→☆☆

Food and occasions

Light, fruity reds make ideal wines for all kinds of summer drinking, such as picnics and barbecues. They also make a good accompaniment for "meaty" fish like salmon and tuna or with pizza and ligher pasta dishes.

GRENACHE – France

This is one of those grape varieties that can be made into very different styles of wine. If Grenache is allowed to produce prolific amounts of grapes it makes light strawberry flavoured wines like basic COTES DU RHONE. If yields are restricted or the resulting wine is oaked it can be a real bruiser. Price is the best guide. Cheap Grenache is likely to taste light (though even then it can be surprisingly alcoholic). Moderately priced or expensive Grenache is much more full-bodied. ☆→☆☆

LAMBRUSCO

Real red Lambrusco is worlds away from the sweet, tasteless white variety that most people identify with this wine. Hovering between still and sparkling, it is exuberantly fruity with a tart red berry flavour.

It's well worth looking in Italian delicatessens and wine merchants with good Italian lists for the more traditional style of Lambrusco rather than the sweeter, more commercial, versions you find in supermarkets. ☆

LOIRE

The Loire Valley is Europe's most northerly red wine-producing area which gives its reds a particularly distinctive character. Broadly they're characterized by a purity of fruit and a marked lack of sweetness that means that even in a good vintage they taste comparatively light. Among the wines made from CABERNET FRANC there is often a herbaceous note, a hint of green pepper, and a curious slatiness that gives them a slightly austere, astringent quality. But it's always accompanied by a lightness and elegance that makes them particularly beguiling. (Unfortunately the fervent following they have gained among wine-lovers – particularly Parisian ones – has resulted in high prices but, unlike other classic French wines, they rarely disappoint.)

The three best-known wines are **Bourgueil**, **Chinon**, and **Saumur-Champigny** which are all based on Cabernet Franc. Chinon tends to be the softest, and fruitiest of the three; Bourgueil and Saumur-Champigny have the greater ageing capacity (up to ten years from the best producers).

The other major Loire red is **Sancerre Rouge**, much less well-known than its white counterpart, a delicate, silky strawberry-flavoured wine which is made from PINOT NOIR. Less expensive Loire reds to look out for include Anjou-Villages, Saumur, and Gamay de Touraine. ☆☆→☆☆☆

MARCILLAC

Increasingly fashionable red wine from the Aveyron which has ridden on the back of the popularity of southwest French cuisine. The majority of wines, which are made from the Fer (Mansois) grape, are juicy and attractively fragrant. ☆☆

MERLOT – unoaked

Normally associated with a much richer, fuller style of wine, inexpensive European Merlot can be quite light-bodied. That is particularly the case in northern Italy where light, fruity quaffing wines such as **Merlot del Veneto** are sometimes as low as 11.5 degrees alcohol. Cheap Merlots from Hungary and from the **Languedoc** also offer simple fruity drinking. ☆→☆☆

MONTEPULCIANO D'ABRUZZO

A smoothly fruity, quaffing wine from central Italy. The cheapest bottles can be rather weak and weedy, but be prepared to pay a little more and you should get a wine that's attractively juicy and supple. ☆→☆☆

PINOT NOIR

With many New World producers now making Pinot Noir in a riper, more full-bodied style it's generally the least expensive pinots that fall into this category. (Not that cheap Pinot is cheap.) That includes most basic Bourgogne Rouge, some of which can be quite sharp, Chilean Pinot Noir which is characterised by its soft raspberry fruit, and the cheapest New Zealand and Californian Pinot Noirs, though both the latter tend to be much sweeter than red burgundy. An exception is Alsace Pinot Noir which tends, whatever the price, to be delicate in taste. Lighter styles of Pinot Noir can also be found in Switzerland, Austria, and Germany (where it is known as Spätburgunder) though again these tend to be pricey, in the UK at least. ☆→☆☆

SANGIOVESE – Italian

As the mainstay of **Chianti** (*see* next section), Sangiovese usually counts as a medium-bodied, if not a heavyweight wine, but where it has been released as a varietal, for example as **Sangiovese di Romana** or **Sangiovese di Toscana**, it's often just a simple light, quaffable red. ☆→☆☆

SARDINIA & SICILY

 Two regions that have improved dramatically in quality over the last few years but can still offer simple basic reds at a bargain price. Wines simply labelled "Sicilian red" are the most likely to be made in this style rather than the blends of native and international varietals such as Nero d'Avola/Shiraz which tend to be more full-bodied. Monica de Sardegna is an attractive light Sardinian red. ☆

TARRANGO

 A recently introduced Australian grape variety which makes vividly fruity, soft sweetish reds – very similar in style to a BEAUJOLAIS. Almost all of it is produced by Brown Brothers of Victoria. ☆☆

TEMPRANILLO – young, unoaked

 Young Tempranillo, known as **Tempranillo Joven** in **Rioja** and **Navarra** is a far cry from the sweetly pruney wines that emerge after months of oak-ageing. Even so it can be quite big and robust and only just falls into this category on the grounds of the sheer vivacity of its fruit. In **La Mancha** and **Valdepeñas** the same grape is known as Cencibel. ☆→☆☆

TEROLDEGO ROTALIANO

 A soft, smooth red produced in the Trentino region of northeast Italy. Rather more like a Swiss or Austrian than an Italian red with intense fruit and less marked acidity. ☆

VALPOLICELLA

Gross commercialisation has in the past disguised the fact that Valpolicella can be a really delightful wine: full and generous with a distinctive ripe cherry flavour. In theory at least, wines labelled "Classico" should be of better quality. "Superiore" means they must be at least twelve degrees of alcohol. Don't buy the cheapest. ☆→☆☆

VIN DE PAYS

The description "*vin de pays*" on a label doesn't necessarily mean the wine inside the bottle is light and fruity, but given that most of these wines are relatively inexpensive, there's a fairly good chance that it will be. The main exception are wines labelled **Vin de Pays d'Oc**. Most of these are made from a single grape variety and in a more full-bodied New World style. ☆→☆☆

VINI DA TAVOLA

Most inexpensive Italian reds, often simply described as a "*vino da tavola*", are light and fruity with a characteristic crisp (and occasionally sharp) acidity. The majority come from the north of the country – particularly from the Veneto. ☆→☆☆

Storing and serving

This is one style of wine that's not really worth keeping for long – more expensive burgundies and Loire reds excepted. Don't be afraid to serve these wines lightly chilled, particularly in the summer.

SMOOTH, MEDIUM-BODIED REDS

Smooth might seem an odd word to use about wine. But the experience of drinking wine is as much about its feel in your mouth as the flavour itself. Many people prefer a wine, particularly a red wine, that is neither too acidic and sharp, as is often the case with lighter wines, or wines that are too strong and alcoholic. This is why this style of wine is so popular.

It includes all the world's best-known wines, from the great French classics of Bordeaux and Burgundy, to the exuberantly fruity reds of Australia and Chile. The big divide is between wines produced in a hot or cool climate.

If you take a grape like Cabernet Sauvignon, for example, in Bordeaux it will make an essentially dry wine, fruity certainly, but not as full and definitely not as sweet as a Cabernet from Chile or South Africa.

How you respond to these contrasting styles depends very much on how long you've been drinking wine and what your starting point is. If the first red wine you drank was Bordeaux and you've been drinking it for twenty years, you may well find a Chilean Cabernet Sauvignon too sweet for your palate. But if you only recently started drinking red wine you would probably find the Chilean Cabernet much more acceptable and a classic Bordeaux too austere.

Old World uncertainties

The challenge with the traditional wine-producing areas is finding wines that are consistently good value. Whereas you can almost guarantee when you buy an inexpensive Australian wine that it will taste like the last bottle you bought, that's much less the case with Bordeaux and Burgundy. The combination of uncertain weather conditions which lead to marked variations in vintage and the fact that the best-known wines are often over-priced means that it's difficult to predict exactly what you're going to get. The best tip is to take advice from a specialist wine shop or a knowledgeable sommelier, but if that isn't possible, follow the guidelines under the entries for each of these regions.

Having said all this, the divisions between the Old World and the New have become a lot less clear cut. Although Burgundy, in the main, remains staunchly traditional, regions like Bordeaux, Chianti, and Rioja have all responded to the demand for softer, fruitier, more approachable reds. In Tuscany, for example, winemakers are adding small amounts of Cabernet to the traditional Sangiovese grape, while those in Spain are increasingly abandoning their old oak casks in favour of new oak barrels. Although this gives rise to criticism that all wines are beginning to taste the same, it's good news for wine-drinkers who may want to widen their choice from the simple fruity flavours of the New World, but are not yet ready to move on to the more distinctive tastes of well-aged wine.

As with most wines, what you get out of this style of wine depends very much on what you are prepared to pay. At the cheaper end of the spectrum, including wines from the south of France and more inexpensive wines from Australia, Chile, and South Africa, the best value is to be found in varietal wines such as Cabernet and Merlot with simple fruit flavours that are ready to drink straight away. If you are prepared to pay more for the wines of, say Bordeaux and Burgundy, you can reasonably expect more complex wines that are capable of maturing over time (though you may still want to drink them within months rather than years). But if you don't like full-bodied reds, avoid those that make a feature of the fact that they have been aged for a considerable time in oak, expecially new oak.

If you like to experiment, look out for the lesser-known appellations of big wine areas like Bordeaux, Burgundy, and the Rhône, for the Beaujolais Crus, for more obscure Spanish and Italian reds, and in the New World for lesser-known grape varieties such as Malbec and Carmenère.

Label Clues

The best indication of whether a red is medium- or full-bodied is the alcohol level. Look out for wines with alcohol levels between 12.5 and 13.5 degrees. Younger vintages generally make lighter drinking. Watch out for the words "reserve" or "reserva" which will tend to indicate a more full-bodied wine.

Starting points	
Smooth and dry	**Sweeter and more fruity**
Bordeaux	Australian Shiraz blends
Chianti Classico	South African Cabernet
Rioja Crianza and Reserva	Chilean Merlot and Carmenère
	New wave Spanish reds

Above *The Médoc region of Bordeaux produces some of the world's most sought-after wines – dry and cedary, with a subtle blackcurrant fruitiness.*

Far left *South African Cabernet Sauvignon generally has a lighter, leaner, less full-bodied character than may of its New World counterparts.*

BEAUJOLAIS – Cru

Although most Beaujolais is light and fruity, the wines named after ten particular districts or villages, the "Crus" (or growths) are generally fuller-bodied. These are **Brouilly**, **Côte de Brouilly**, **Chénas**, **Chiroubles**, **Fleurie**, **Juliénas**, **Morgon**, **Moulin-à-Vent**, **Régnié**, and **St-Amour**. Wines vary from one producer to another, but Chiroubles, Fleurie, and St-Amour are generally lighter, Morgon and Moulin-à-Vent more intense.

☆☆→☆☆☆

BERGERAC and other Bordeaux-style wines

Very similar wines to BORDEAUX, made from the same grape varieties, are produced in the surrounding areas. Bergerac, **Côtes de Duras**, **Côtes du Frontonnais,** and **Côtes du Marmandais** are on a par with basic Bordeaux; CABERNET-dominated **Buzet** tends to be more full-bodied. The Languedoc also produces wines in this style – particularly in **Cabardès** and **Côtes de la Malepère**. ☆→☆☆

BONARDA

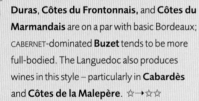

Originally a northern Italian grape variety, Bonarda is popular in Argentina for making rustic, brambly reds. ☆→☆☆

BORDEAUX

Bordeaux is a huge wine area, producing five times as much as BURGUNDY. We tend to think of it in terms of its most famous and illustrious

châteaux, but the vast majority of bottles it produces are classified as basic Bordeaux.

The classic Bordeaux grape varieties are CABERNET SAUVIGNON and MERLOT, with occasionally some Cabernet Franc, MALBEC or Petit Verdot. The two major grapes are perfect partners, the softer Merlot fleshing out the austere, more tannic Cabernet. But in practice, with the increasing demand for soft, fruity wines, it is Merlot that increasingly dominates.

There have also been changes in winemaking. A lot of Bordeaux used to be left to macerate for days and was then aged for months in old oak casks. This meant that even young wines could be impenetrably tough and tannic. Now the emphasis is on accentuating Bordeaux's natural fruitiness, supplemented by new oak so that even the biggest wines tend to be drinkable straight away.

Even then, there is always a dryness and almost savouriness compared to the much sweeter flavour of a New World Cabernet or Merlot – a sensation of lightness on the palate despite the fact that the flavour is full. This is particularly the case with wines with a high proportion of Cabernet.

The two things that help you pin down the style of Bordeaux is what part of the region it is from and from what kind of property (*see* other entries in this section). All labels indicate the area the wine comes from: the more specific that area is, the more complex and expensive the wine is likely to be. ☆→☆☆☆

BORDEAUX AC

Basic Bordeaux – or claret – can come from anywhere in the region and may have been blended from more than one area. Most is simple, young, fruity, and inexpensive.

Bordeaux Supérieur on the label means that it contains more alcohol and should, in theory, be better quality. ☆→☆☆

BURGUNDY

With so many different names and so many different producers, Burgundy is maddeningly difficult to pin down. But what distinguishes its wines is a generous sweetness and softness that belies its often high levels of alcohol. This is PINOT NOIR at its most classic, with an intoxicating purity of flavour, sensuously silky texture, and occasionally a high octane blast of supercharged fruit and spice.

The best starting point is the formal classification system. The two categories that fall into this section are "village wines" (named after the village in which they are produced) and *premiers crus* – better quality village wines to which the name of the vineyard is attached, e.g. Savigny-lès-Beaune-Les Serpentières. *Premiers crus* tend to be more full-bodied and have greater ageing capacity.

Lighter styles include all the "Côtes" and "Villages" – wines which don't carry specific village names, but which may be of decent quality. They include **Bourgogne CÔTE CHALONNAISE**, **Hautes-Côtes de Nuits**, **CÔTE DE NUITS-Villages**, **Hautes-Côtes de Beaune,** and **CÔTE DE BEAUNE-Villages**.

Village wines are the next step up. People tend to be impressed by the best-known names such as **Gevrey-Chambertin** and Nuits-St-Georges in the CÔTE DE NUITS, but the vineyards of a less famous appellation which may literally be just down the road, can offer far better value. The highest classification of *grand cru* for wines which come from the region's best vineyards tend to be more full-bodied and/or rare (see pages 72–7 and 78–81).

All these generalisations, of course, can be affected by the vintage. Burgundy is susceptible to bad weather and the grapes don't always ripen fully. A burgundy from a challenging year like 2001 will generally be less full-bodied than one in a hot vintage like 2003 – though a top producer will still make a better wine in a bad year than a poor producer will in a good one. ☆☆→☆☆☆

CABERNET SAUVIGNON

In warmer climates than those of BORDEAUX and southwest France, Cabernet Sauvignon tends to be much richer and riper, but there are some examples of less full-bodied wines. These include less expensive Cabernets from Bulgaria, Chile, Italy, and the Languedoc. ☆→☆☆☆

CARMENERE

A traditional grape variety from Bordeaux planted widely in Chile and for many years mistaken for Merlot which it strongly resembles. Inexpensive examples are smooth, lush, and fruity. ☆→☆☆

CHIANTI

One of Italy's best-known wines, made in Tuscany from the Sangiovese grape. Like many of the world's most famous wines, the quality of Chianti varies hugely, but most combine rich, plummy fruit with a typically (for Italian wines) high acidity. Within a couple of years

more traditionally made versions develop a sweet, slightly, raisiny, pruney flavour. But, like everywhere else in the wine world, Tuscany is changing and Chianti is increasingly made in a more obviously fruity style, usually by adding a small amount (up to ten per cent) of CABERNET SAUVIGNON, MERLOT or SYRAH to the wine instead of the traditional proportion of white grape varieties. Better quality Chianti comes from one of seven sub-regions, the best-known of which are **Classico** and **Rufina**. ☆→☆☆☆

COTE DE BEAUNE

Although better-known for its whites, this, the southern half of BURGUNDY's Côte d'Or – also produces significant reds including **Aloxe-Corton**, **Pommard**, and **Volnay**, though, in general, the wines are lighter and more supple than those of the COTE DE NUITS. For value try **Auxey-Duresses**, **Monthélie**, **Pernand-Vergelesses**, **Santenay**, **Savigny-lès-Beaune**, and **St-Aubin**. ☆☆

COTE CHALONNAISE

BURGUNDY wine region just to the south of the COTE DE BEAUNE producing wines that offer comparatively good value for the region. Look out for **Givry**, **Mercurey**, and **Rully** (particularly on restaurant wine lists). ☆☆

COTE DE NUITS

The part of the Côte d'Or where most top red BURGUNDIES are produced. Some, like **Nuits-St-Georges** and **Gevrey-Chambertin**, are (or should be) more full-bodied and fall into the

Food and occasions

The occasion and your choice of guests are likely to be the most important factors determining your choice of wine. More traditional wines like Bordeaux, burgundy, and Rioja are better for more formal occasions and older guests; modern varietals like Cabernet and Merlot tend to be better for informal parties and a younger age group. The same division extends to food. Old World wines suit the more classic cuisines of France and Italy; New World wines, more spicy, adventurous flavours.

next section. Others, like **Chambolle - Musigny** and **Vosne-Romanée,** are lighter, lusher, and more supple. **Fixin** and **Marsannay** offer great value . ☆☆→☆☆☆

COTES DU RHONE-VILLAGES

Full and fruity, these are generally much more substantial than basic Côtes du Rhône. If the village name, such as **Cairanne, Valréas,** or **Sablet** is given on the label, the quality is likely to be higher still. ☆☆

CROZES-HERMITAGE – and other medium-bodied Rhône reds

Some of the less expensive Rhône appellations such as Crozes-Hermitage, **Gigondas, Lirac,** and **St-Joseph** are also capable of producing generously fruity reds, but without the weight of a **Cornas** of a **Châteauneuf-du-Pape.** Another name to look out for is **Costières de Nîmes,** technically in the Languedoc, but making vigorously fruity reds similar to those of the Rhône. ☆☆

CRUS BOURGEOIS

An official ranking of châteaux in the MEDOC which, while in theory less prestigious than the **Crus Classés** (the first five growths – *see* page 80) are still highly rated. It was overhauled in 2003 and divided into three levels of Crus Bourgeois Exceptionnel which includes only nine châteaux, Crus Bourgeois Supérieur, and Crus Bourgeois. Other Bordeaux to look out for are those referred to by wine merchants as **Petits Châteaux** – wines that miss out on the

official classification system but can offer solid, reliable drinking. ☆☆→☆☆☆

FRONSAC

A good example of a Bordeaux appellation that (along with neighbouring **Canon-Fronsac**) offers better value than some of the household names. Just next door to ST-EMILION, its wines share the same soft, fruity character. Other underrated appellations on the "Right Bank" include **Côtes de Castillon, Côtes de Francs,** and **Côtes de Bourg.** ☆☆

HAUT-MEDOC

A region made famous by its four best known communes – **Margaux, St-Julien, Pauillac,** and **St-Estèphe,** which contain most of BORDEAUX'S most celebrated châteaux. Less well-known are the communes of **Moulis** and **Listrac** which are frequently the source of excellent wines. ☆☆→☆☆☆

MEDOC & GRAVES

The two BORDEAUX appellations that sandwich the more prestigious HAUT-MEDOC on the Left Bank of the Gironde make a slightly lighter, fruitier style of Bordeaux. These days MERLOT tends to dominate, rather than the more traditional CABERNET SAUVIGNON. ☆☆→☆☆☆

MALBEC – Argentina and Chile

This variety is successful in the Mendoza region of Argentina, producing soft, fleshy

reds with ripe, smooth, plummy fruit, some of which fall into the next section (*see* page 77). A similar style of wine is made in Chile. ☆

MERLOT

There's a fundamental sweetness and generosity about Merlot that ensures that even the most concentrated, expensively oaked wines are smoothly enjoyable. The most elegant examples undoubtedly come from BORDEAUX, but serious wines are also to be found in Chile, South Africa, and California. By and large, the more inexpensive bottles tend to be softer and sweeter than wines which are bolstered by oak. If you prefer a lighter style, try inexpensive Merlot from Chile or South Africa, Chile has the most lushly fruity Merlots, California the most concentrated. ☆→☆☆

MOURVEDRE/MATARO

This grape variety has an aromatic, perfumed quality which isn't immediately obvious in such full-bodied wines as **Bandol** (or in Spain where it is called Monastrell), but which plays a significant part in many southern French reds such as **Faugères.** As Mataro, the name normally used in Australia, it can produce simple, juicy, fruity reds. ☆☆→☆☆☆

NAVARRA – and modern Spanish reds

Spain is currently one of the most exciting countries of the wine world, producing some extraordinarily vibrant fruity reds. Less expensive bottles from such areas as Navarra,

Costers del Segre, Penedès, Tarragona, and Utiel Requena fall into this category, though many modern Spanish reds are more full-bodied (*see pages 72–77*). ☆→☆☆

PINOT NOIR – New World, oaked

The majority of high-quality New World Pinot Noir falls into this category, even when it is labelled "Reserve". That includes most Pinots from California and Oregon, from New Zealand, from newcomers Canada and New York State, and from the cooler regions of Australia such as the Yarra Valley, Mornington Peninsula, and Tasmania. ☆☆→☆☆☆

RIOJA – modern style

Although Rioja is traditionally identified with a more mature style of wine (*see pages 78–81*), producers are increasingly ignoring the traditional classification of Reserva and Gran Reserva, which necessitates the wines spending several years in oak, and producing more youthful, fruity styles. Apart from the vintage, clues to look out for on a label are the words **joven** (young) or **Tempranillo** (the main grape variety used in Rioja) which do not normally appear on more traditional wines. The description **crianza** which states the wine has spent twelve months in wood usually indicates a medium-bodied style. ☆☆

ROSSO DI MONTALCINO – and other Italian reds

Two good alternatives to more expensive Tuscan reds are Rosso di Montalcino and

Rosso di Montepulciano – less grand versions of **Brunello di Montalcino** and **Vino Nobile di Montepulciano** respectively. From the Marches, **Rosso Conero** and **Rosso Piceno** both offer good value while some of the better quality wines among the northern Italian reds mentioned in the last section, such as **Barbera** and **Valpolicella**, can also make relatively robust drinking. ☆☆

RUBY CABERNET

A cross of CABERNET SAUVIGNON and Carignan producing far from subtle, but richly fruity reds. It often acts as a useful blending partner for cheaper wines in the New World, especially in California, South Africa and, to a lesser extent, Australia. ☆

ST-EMILION & POMEROL

Ultra-fashionable BORDEAUX appellations producing some of the region's most lush, supple (and, regrettably, expensive) wines with superstars **Pétrus** and **Le Pin**. Unlike the MEDOC, better wines are designated *grand cru classé* and *premier grand cru classé* (the former offer better value). Bargains can also be found in "satellite" villages such as **Montagne-St-Emilion** and **Lussac-St-Emilion**. ☆☆→☆☆☆

SHIRAZ BLENDS – Australia

Although Australian Shiraz is generally robust and full-bodied, cheaper blends with grapes such as CABERNET SAUVIGNON and Ruby CABERNET generally make easy-drinking. ☆

Storing and serving

The less-expensive wines in this style are designed to be drunk relatively quickly, usually within the year. More expensive wines will last a good deal longer, though if you want to avoid them beginning to taste like a well-matured wine, you would do best to drink them within a couple of years. Bigger, more expensive wines also repay opening an hour before serving, unlike cheaper wines which can be poured straight away.

FULL-BODIED REDS

Wine-drinkers rarely start off liking full-bodied reds, but there are few dedicated wine enthusiasts who don't end up loving them. This is as winey as wine gets: intense, concentrated, and richly satisfying.

It's an increasingly common style, it used to be rare for winemakers to make reds of over fourteen per cent ABV but it's now quite common place even in the more traditional wine-producing countries of Europe. Hotter summers and a tendency to pick grapes later and riper have both contributed. Certain grape varieties also lend themselves more to more full-bodied wines. Cabernet Sauvignon, with its small, thick-skinned grapes, is capable of making deeply coloured wines with a high level of tannin. The same is true of Nebbiolo, the intensely tannic grape used for the great Italian wines Barolo and Barbaresco, and of many of the Portuguese varieties such as Touriga Nacional, Touriga Francesca, and Tinta Barocca, which are also used for making port.

Ripe, concentrated wines

The world's best wines also tend to be richly concentrated. They are often produced from grapes from low-yielding vines usually grown on infertile, rocky soils where the vines have to dig deep in order to get nourishment.

Such wines also get special treatment in the winery, including leaving the juice in contact with the skins for as long as possible and fermenting at higher than average temperatures to extract maximum colour and flavour. The resulting wine is then aged in good quality oak to give it extra structure and longevity. All this helps to explain why many full-bodied wines are so costly; they are expensive to make.

The great hunting grounds for these wines are the Rhône, northwest and Southern Italy, and Australia. The easiest to get to grips with is Australia, whose rich, full-bodied Cabernet, Grenache, and Shiraz wines have a lush sweetness that offsets their intensity. It is sometimes hard to believe that Syrah from the Rhône is the same grape variety as Shiraz from Australia. Though full-bodied and spicy, Rhône Syrah's fruit is much less obvious and the wines often have a gamey quality. Yet the Rhône's top wines, such as Hermitage, Cornas, and Côte Rôtie, are among the finest in the world.

The great wines of Piedmont in the northwest of Italy, Barolo and Barbaresco, are also quite an acquired taste. Though they are less tannic than they once were, they can take years to open up. Top Tuscan wines may be less of a challenge, but they are as expensive as top Bordeaux or burgundy. Many of Sicily's best reds are also made in a rich full-bodied style.

For everyday drinking, good value can be found in the traditional appellations of the Languedoc, such as Corbières, Fitou, Minervois, and St-Chinian which blend Syrah with the other classic southern French varieties of Grenache, Mourvèdre, and Carignan. Modern Spanish reds such as Jumilla and those from Toro are also reasonably priced – with the exeption of Priorat. And there are also some wonderfully individual wines from Portugal and the Douro region in particular.

Elsewhere in the New World it is Cabernet Sauvignon that provides the most well-trodden route to this type of drinking, particularly in California (where they take it very seriously indeed), Washington State, and Chile – which is producing some magificent Bordeaux-style reds. Malbec and Syrah from Argentia are other rewarding wines to explore.

Wines vary with respect to how long they keep their full-bodied character before falling into the next category of aged, more mature wines. The more concentrated they are, the longer they retain their original character. I have drunk modestly priced Australian reds that have retained their intensity for eight to ten years. But some wines from a cooler climate or a less good vintage may lose their power after four or five years.

Label clues

A high alcohol content of 13.5 to 14.5 degrees is obviously the major clue to wines of this style. Some even reach fifteen degrees. Look out also for the word "reserve" on the label, which usually indicates the wine has spent a substantial time in oak, and for wines that are unfiltered (see pages 26–31).

Starting points	
Old World	**New World**
Fitou and other Langedoc reds	Australian and South African Shiraz
Châteauneuf-du-Pape	Top New World Cabernet
Nero d'Avola	South African Pinotage
Toro	Zinfandel

Above *Châteauneuf-du-Pape is the best-known appellation in the southern Rhône in France, producing potent, spicy, fruity reds.*

Far left *The Barossa valley in South Australia is one of Australia's longest established wine-growing regions, producing particularly rich, full-bodied examples of shiraz.*

BANDOL

Fashionable, small Provençal appellation whose richly flavoured, slightly gamey reds, based on the exotic Mourvèdre grape, can command hefty prices. The wines, which are aged for at least eighteen months in wood should last at least ten years. ☆☆→☆☆☆

BAROLO & BARBARESCO

Despite a significant degree of modernization, Barolo is still one of the most traditionally produced of wines: dense and plummy with unfashionably high levels of tannin. Made from the Nebbiolo grape in Piedmont in the northwest of Italy, it often spends three to five years in cask and can take several years to reach its peak, when it develops a magnificent, deep chocolatey intensity. More expensive wines are labelled with the names of the individual towns or villages they come from: Barolo itself, Castiglione Falletto, La Morra, Monforte, and Serralunga. Barbaresco, Piedmont's other great red, is similar in style though can be more approachable. ☆☆→☆☆☆

BURGUNDY

Although most burgundy is more light-bodied than this, the best wines, from the best producers, can be intensely rich and concentrated. This is true, at their best, of well-known wines like Gevrey-Chambertin and Nuits-St-Georges, and of smaller appellations like Pommard, Volnay, and Vosne-Romanée, especially if drunk young. ☆☆☆

CABERNET FRANC

A grape that typically makes more fragrant, lighter reds. But wines from New World countries and regions such as Chile and California tend to be much richer and more structured. ☆☆

CABERNET SAUVIGNON – New World

This grape variety is so widely planted that it is made in a huge variety of styles. The presence of two factors determine whether it is full-bodied or not – a reliably warm or hot climate and the use of oak. Most of the moderately priced and more expensive New World Cabernets from countries such as Australia, California, and South Africa are full-bodied, as are the top-quality Cabernets from Spanish and Italian producers. Even some Bordeaux producers now make full-bodied wines. Reliably full-bodied Cabernets come from:

Australia Both the Barossa and McLaren Vale in South Australia produce some stunning wines, but the most distinctive Cabernets come from the Coonawarra, whose unique "terra rossa" soil gives a pronounced mint and eucalyptus character. The cooler Margaret River region of Western Australia produces more classic European-style wines, but still with an intensity of flavour that is typically Australian. ☆☆→☆☆☆☆

California Some of the most intense, concentrated Cabernets in the world are made in northern California, particularly in the Napa Valley where the fruit is riper and oak influence more marked than in Bordeaux. ☆☆→☆☆☆☆

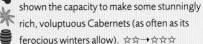

Washington State A strong pretender to California's throne, this region has already shown the capacity to make some stunningly rich, voluptuous Cabernets (as often as its ferocious winters allow). ☆☆→☆☆☆☆

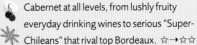

Chile Chile has had huge success in producing Cabernet at all levels, from lushly fruity everyday drinking wines to serious "Super-Chileans" that rival top Bordeaux. ☆→☆☆☆

New Zealand New Zealand has overcome initial difficulties in ripening Cabernet and is now producing reliably ripe wines from warmer areas such as Hawkes Bay, often blended with Merlot. ☆☆→☆☆☆☆

South Africa Less consistent in the past than some of its fellow New World wine-producing countries. But, at the top end of the scale, there are wines of considerable elegance, especially from Stellenbosch. ☆→☆☆☆

CAHORS

The reputation of Cahors wines, some of the most full-bodied and tannic in the southwest of France, goes back to the thirteenth century. Based on the Malbec grape (referred to locally as Auxerrois), they were at one time so dense and dark, they were referred to as "black wine", and were often used to beef up basic Bordeaux. Now blended more extensively with Merlot, many producers are making their wines in a lighter, more supple style. ☆☆

CARIGNAN

A formerly despised workhorse of a grape variety planted throughout Spain (as Cariñena) and southern France and the backbone of many of its dark, dense traditional reds. However old vine Carignan is now undergoing something of a renaissance and is increasingly being bottled on its own. One of the best versions comes from Sardinia: the dark, damsony **Carignano del Sulcis**. There's also some interest in this grape in Chile and California. ☆→☆☆

CHATEAUNEUF-DU-PAPE

The best-known appellation of the southern Rhône; a rich, spicy red based on GRENACHE (though up to thirteen different grape varieties including some whites, can be used). Cheaper versions can seem lightweight, though deceptively so. The alcohol content is always high.

Better quality wines (which almost invariably come from individual estates such as Château de Beaucastel and Vieux Télégraphe) benefit from several years' ageing. ☆☆→☆☆☆

COLLIOURE

A tiny French appellation, virtually on the Spanish border, producing fine, full, spicy reds based on GRENACHE and Mourvèdre that are among the very best from Roussillon. ☆☆

CORNAS

Small, northern Rhône appellation producing savoury, dense, long-lived 100 per cent Syrah wines that can compete with HERMITAGE on the opposite bank – and occasionally surpass it for value. ☆☆☆

COTE ROTIE

The most expensive and feted of the Rhône's reds, Côte Rôtie undoubtedly produces some of the most excitingly sensuous wines in the world, combining rich concentration with an extraordinary degree of suppleness. Though predominately made from Syrah, producers may include a small amount of the aromatic white Viognier grape which adds to the wine's heady, seductive bouquet. Scarcity combined with demand has resulted in some frightening prices for these wines. ☆☆☆

DOURO and other Portuguese reds

Portugal offers some of the most individual full-bodied reds in the world, especially from the port-producing area of the Douro where the same grapes are used to make increasingly sought-after table wines. Quality in other areas such as Dão and Bairrada has also markedly improved resulting in much more vibrant, less oaky wines. ☆☆→☆☆☆

GRENACHE/GARNACHA

Mature Grenache (or Garnacha in Spain) vines produce wines with an extraordinary degree of concentration, the virtues of which

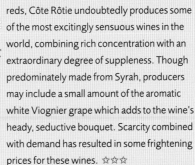

Food and occasions

These are obviously not wines that are suited to light, summer drinking, though cheaper bottles can be great with a barbecue. Classic European wines like those from Piedmont and the Rhône go well with substantial French and Italian meat dishes, particularly game or beef. New World Cabernets and Australian Shiraz can handle spicier flavours. All are ideal for warming cold weather food, but are perhaps better saved for fellow red wine enthusiasts than guests whose taste in wine you're unfamiliar with.

the Australians have belatedly recognized after pulling up some of their oldest vines. Increasingly it is being blended with Shiraz and Mourvèdre (Mataro) as in the Rhône. Garnacha is also celebrated in some of the best new Spanish reds from Priorat, Monsant, and Taragona. ☆☆

HERMITAGE

Arguably the world's most famous full-bodied red and the model for Syrah in both the Old and New World. (Hermitage was the name originally used in Australia for SHIRAZ.) The densest, most concentrated of the northern Rhône appellations, the wines are seldom drinkable under five years and generally better left for ten or more. ☆☆☆

JUMILLA

A hot, dry area of southern Spain producing rich, dark, high-alcohol reds from the Monastrell (**Mourvèdre**) grape. Traditionally used for blending, more modern winemaking techniques have resulted in some attractively lush, fruity wines. ☆→☆☆

LANGUEDOC

Though they are made over a wide geographical area, there is a strong family resemblance between the reds of the Languedoc, with differences frequently being more marked between one producer and another than between appellations. The most robust wines are from poorer schistous soils and producers who use a higher proportion of

CARIGNAN: primarily the **Fitou** and **St-Chinian** areas. Other producers who use a higher proportion of GRENACHE, Syrah, and Mourvèdre such as those in the **Faugères** and **Minervois**, often make more elegant wines. **Corbières**, the biggest region, produces a wide range of styles, but many producers still age their wines for some considerable time in oak which makes them among the more full-bodied choices.

Things change fast in the Languedoc, though, due to the combination of lack of regulation and the large number of foreign winemakers working in the region. Many of the more ambitious and dynamic producers are now electing to produce their wines as **Coteaux du Languedoc** or a vin de pays rather than one of the more traditional appellations. Look out also for the full-bodied wines of Pic St-Loup. ☆→☆☆

MALBEC

Increasingly popular among winemakers in Argentina and Chile who coax rich plummy flavours out of this traditional French grape variety. *See also* CAHORS. ☆☆

NEGROAMARO & NERO D'AVOLA

Two fascinating indigenous red grape varieties from Puglia and Sicily respectively that are helping to contribute to the improved quality of southern Italian wines. Traditionally they produced aged, figgy reds but are now used on their own or in blends with international varieties such as Syrah to make much more vibrant, brambly full-flavoured wines. ☆→☆☆☆

PETITE SIRAH

Increasingly fashionable grape variety in California where old vines are used to make sturdy, spicy reds. Also grown in Australia where it is known as Durif. ☆→☆☆

PETIT VERDOT

Obscure but fashionable Bordeaux grape variety taken up by Australian and a few other winemakers to produce inky-dark, plummy reds. ☆→☆☆

PINOTAGE

This indigenous South African grape, a blend of PINOT NOIR and Cinsault, is capable of making magnificently dense, plummy wines from low-yielding old vines. Best examples represent tremendous value. ☆☆

PINOT NOIR

Although Pinot Noir would not generally be thought of as a full-bodied wine, full-bodied examples regularly come from specific producers and regions such as Geelong in Australia and Central Otago in New Zealand. ☆

PRIORATO/PRIORAT

Expensive and much fêted, this Grenache-based Spanish wine reaches hefty levels of alcohol. ☆☆☆

RIBERA DEL DUERO

 Prestigious Spanish wine-growing region producing mainly Tempranillo-based wines (here called Tinto Fino) which tend to be more full-bodied, savoury, and gamey than Rioja. Also home to famous and fashionable wines such as Vega Sicilia and Pingus (see page 81) which use a proportion of international grapes such as Cabernet Sauvignon and Merlot. ☆☆☆

SHIRAZ/SYRAH

 Two different faces of the same grape variety, Shiraz and Syrah seem designed to indulge the lover of full-bodied reds. Syrah is the name they use in the northern Rhône where it is produces such great long-lived wines as Cornas and Hermitage. California and Argentina also use the Syrah name – their wines tend to be sweeter and lusher with less of the classic black pepper character that characterizes the Rhône.

In South Australia, especially in the Barossa Valley, it produces fabulously sweet lush wines, that age over time to a savoury richness. In the Hunter Valley it has more of a savoury character, developing more animal, gamey notes, sometimes described as "sweaty saddle", while Shiraz from cooler Western Australia is more elegant, with smooth red berry fruit, not unlike a Cabernet. South Africa also leans towards the South Australian style, producing big, bold, fruity reds which they also call Shiraz rather than Syrah and there are some powerful examples from Argentina. ☆☆→☆☆☆

TANNAT

 Appropriately named tannic grape variety widely used to make dark, dense reds in Uruguay. Also the backbone of French Madiran, a full-bodied wine from southwest Fance. ☆☆

TORO

 Up and coming central Spanish wine region producing vivid, exciting, muscular reds. ☆☆

VINO NOBILE DE MONTEPULCIANO

 A smooth, sophisticated Tuscan wine made primarily from the Sangiovese grape. A cheaper alternative to **Brunello di Montalcino**. ☆☆

ZINFANDEL/PRIMITIVO

 Zinfandel in the hands of small artisanal winemakers produces wines of great power and personality which have attracted a cult following. Established in California during the last century, it has been discovered to be the same variety as Italian Primitivo, though the latter is generally not of the same calibre. The best growing areas are in northern California in the Dry Creek and Alexander Valleys, the Sierra Foothills, and Paso Robles to the south of San Francisco which still retain many old vines. ☆☆→☆☆☆☆

Storing and serving

Most full-bodied wines will survive for at least a couple of years in average domestic conditions and in the case of more expensive wines, a good five to eight years. Some like the top Rhône and Italian wines need that amount of time before they even start to be drinkable. Open them at least an hour, preferably two, before serving them, or even decant them beforehand.

AGED RED WINES AND RARITIES

One of the biggest changes in the wine world is how soon we now drink a bottle of red wine after we've bought it. Traditionally, any remotely serious red wine was always "laid down" and no-one would have dreamt of drinking it young. Nowadays, even expensive wines are designed to be drunk straight off the shelf with the result that the taste of mature wine is quite unfamiliar, not to say unappealing, to many wine-drinkers.

The taste is indeed very different. Instead of the vivid fruit and robust tannins of a young wine, the texture and flavour become softer and less assertive. Simple blackcurrant or raspberry fruit gives way to the more autumnal flavours of prunes and plums, and even all kinds of unlikely aromas and flavours. A mature burgundy, for example, can have distinctly "farmyardy" aromas, a smell of wet undergrowth or frequently of truffles or mushrooms, a quality much prized by burgundy aficionados, but one that can come as quite a shock first time around.

Wine lives and breathes

Why this happens is that unlike other packaged food and drink products wine continues evolving in the bottle. After bottling there is always a small amount of oxygen left which reacts with the phenols in the wine (the compounds in the stems, skins, pips, and pulp of grapes which give wine colour and structure) which eventually cluster together to form a sediment which drops to the bottom of the bottle. (This is why older red wines fade in colour and become less tannic.)

Of course this doesn't happen to all wines – or all wines at the same rate. Fruity, unoaked reds that are designed to be drunk young, simply become dull and flat-tasting. There's no point in keeping a Beaujolais Nouveau. Some grapes age better than others: Syrah and Shiraz, for example, will generally outlive Pinot Noir. Cabernet Sauvignon has more staying power than Merlot. But even Cabernet varies in its capacity to age depending on where and how it is made (see listing).

In cooler regions, such as Bordeaux and Burgundy, the longevity of a wine also relates to the quality of the vintage. In a good year, the grapes ripen fully and the resulting wines are more concentrated and age better than thinner wines of a poor vintage, though this distinction is becoming blurred by modern winemaking techniques.

But the most significant factor is how concentrated a wine is in the first place – and that is almost always reflected in its price. As a general rule, cheaper wines show their age more quickly than expensive ones as do wines, lilke Rioja, which ave spent a considerable time in oak. It also depends on the oak that is used. Wines aged in old oak casks will taste softer and more mellow than wine that is aged in new oak barrels, which impart a lusher texture and a more lively vanilla flavour.

In fact, people are more likely to come to grief from letting wines age for too long than by drinking them too quickly. In centrally heated flats and houses, wines rarely benefit from being kept for more than two or three years. It is only so-called "fine wines" that are worth keeping for any longer than that – and that assumes ideal storage conditions (*see* pages 110–13). Among them would be included wines from Bordeaux, Burgundy, and the Rhône, more expensive Italian reds from Tuscany and Piedmont, and top wines from California and Australia. Many won't even begin to show at their best for five years or more.

That doesn't mean if you have a taste for mature wine but are without a pocket to match that you can't indulge yourself. Spain, in particular, is a good hunting ground for reasonably priced oak-aged reds, most notably Rioja and Ribera del Duero, but also Navarra and Valdepeñas. The same is true of wines like Copertino and Salice Salentino from southern Italy. But do drink them straight off the shelf.

Also included here are some of the wine world's most quirky and individual reds – wines like Aglianico del Vulture and the great Lebanese wine Château Musar. Given their rarity, they are very reasonably priced, but not to everyone's taste. Save them for fellow enthusiasts.

Label clues

The most obvious indication that a wine is mature is that it comes from an older vintage, but unless you are confident of your source be wary of buying any inexpensive or moderately priced wine over five years old. Look out for the words "*reserve*", "*riserva*" or "*reserva*" which indicate an oak-aged wine intended to be matured.

Above *Harvesting in the Bekaa Valley which produces the grapes for Château Musar – the finest Lebanese wine – a rich, full-bodied blend of Cabernet Sauvignon, Cinsault, and Syrah.*

Far left *The sort of cellar wine-lovers dream about. Haut-Brion is one of the Bordeaux greats.*

Starting points	
Aged wines	**Rarities**
Valdepeñas	Amarone
Salice Salentino	Aglianico del Vulture
Rioja Reserva or Gran Reserva	Château Musar

AGLIANICO DEL VULTURE

One of the lesser-known but great full-bodied Italian reds made down in the very south of Italy from the late-ripening Aglianico grape. ☆☆

AMARONE

A unique off-dry, almost port-like red of great richness and concentration made in the Valpolicella region in northeastern Italy from the local Corvina, Rondinella, and Molinara grape varieties. It can be drunk with rich meat and game dishes but with at least fourteen degrees of alcohol is probably more suitable as an accompaniment for cheese.
☆☆→☆☆☆

BARCA VELHA

Cult Portuguese red from the Douro region, made from the same grape varieties as port and released only in an exceptional year (*see* other Douro reds page 76). ☆☆☆

BORDEAUX – *crus classés*

Not all of the sixty-one wines of the officially recognised top growths of the Médoc qualify for this section on grounds of rarity, but the fact is that most of us will get to drink a wine like Château Latour or Mouton Rothschild once in a lifetime – if that. Certainly it's worth being able to recognise the names of the five first growths – **Haut-Brion**, **Lafite-Rothschild**, **Latour**, **Margaux**, and **Mouton-Rothschild** – together with the two Pomerol superstars,

Châteaux Pétrus and **Le Pin** – so you can appreciate just what you're being offered if anyone opens one up for you. The so-called "*garagiste*" wines so popular in the 1990s are less in favour now. ☆☆☆

BOLGHERI

Much lauded new Tuscan sub-region. Home to Italy's cultish wines Sassicaia and Ornellaia, the original Super-Tuscans. ☆☆☆

BRUNELLO DI MONTALCINO

An elegant and expensive Tuscan wine, Italy's equivalent to the top Bordeaux growths is made from Brunello, a variant of the Sangiovese grape. Like other top Italian reds, it spends a substantial time in oak and isn't released until it is at least four years old. Good vintages will last for decades. ☆☆☆

CABERNET SAUVIGNON – mature

Because of its basically tough, tannic character Cabernet Sauvignon is one of the grape varieties best suited to ageing, as top winemakers have amply demonstrated in both the Old and New World. The rate at which this happens, however, differs quite markedly. Cheaper Cabernets from South Africa for instance will develop the typically soft, pruney flavour of mature Cabernet within three to four years of bottling. But more expensive Australian and Californian Cabernets which have an intense concentration of fruit, may not develop that kind of character for eight to ten years.
☆☆→☆☆☆

CHATEAU MUSAR

The most distinguished red wine of the Lebanon which continued to be produced throughout the civil war. This is a long-lived, powerful, yet elegant blend of Cabernet Sauvignon, Cinsault, and Syrah, which bears comparison with many far more expensive BORDEAUX wines. ☆☆

CHIANTI CLASSICO RISERVA

The ageing requirements for Chianti Classico and other Riserva Chiantis have now been reduced from three to two years, but *riservas* should still be significantly longer-lived than basic Chianti. The top wines from such producers as Antinori and Isole e Olena can age for up to thirty years. ☆☆→☆☆☆

GARRAFEIRA – Portugal

An indication of quality in Portuguese wines denoting that the wine is from an exceptional vintage, has been aged for two years in oak, and for a further year in the bottle. ☆☆

GRANGE

Along with Henschke's Hill of Grace, Australia's most sought-after Shiraz, a wine first produced in the 1950s (as Grange Hermitage) in an attempt to emulate BORDEAUX's first growths. It does, in fact, taste more like a mature CABERNET SAUVIGNON. ☆☆☆

NEGROAMARO

 You can almost taste the hot sun in the wines: there's a kind of baked, caramelized flavour to them, which is saved from being bitter by a delicious brown sugar fudginess. Most are based on the Negroamaro (literally "black and bitter") grape combined with Malvasia Nera. Names to look out for include **Copertino**, **Salice Salentino,** and **Squinzano**. ☆→☆☆

PRIORATO

 A small denomination in the Spanish province of Catalonia producing intensely concentrated, alcoholic wines (the minimum alcohol content is 13.75) from low-yielding Garnacha (Grenache) and Cariñena (Carignan) vines. *See also* page 77. ☆☆☆

RIOJA RESERVA/GRAN RESERVA

 Prolonged ageing in oak makes mature *reserva* and *gran reserva* Rioja some of the most obviously oaky wines available, their typical soft strawberry jam fruit giving way over time to more complex gamey flavours.

Reserva indicates that the wine will have been aged for three years before release, at least one of which will have been spent in oak; *gran reserva* is only released after five years, two of them in oak. ☆☆→☆☆☆

LA ROMANEE-CONTI

 The production of Burgundy's most celebrated wines like La Romanée-Conti, **Richebourg** and **La Tâche** is so minute that almost every bottle is spoken for before the grapes are harvested (La Romanée-Conti is a single-vineyard less than two hectares in size). There are other *grands crus* such as **Bonnes Mares**, **Corton,** and **Echézeaux** which are easier to get hold of – if you can afford them. ☆☆☆

SALICE SALENTINO

 One of the best known of southern Italy's (Puglia) traditional reds which tastes like a well-matured wine – even when young. Made from the Negroamaro grape (*see also* page 76), there's a warm sun-baked quality to the fruit that makes them quite distinctive. Look out too for **Copertino** and **Squinzano**. ☆→☆☆

SCREAMING EAGLE

 One of California's legendary cult Cabernet producers along with others such as Harlan and Grace Family Vineyard. Ultra concentrated and ultra expensive. ☆☆☆

VALDEPENAS

 A reasonably priced source of traditional Spanish oak-aged reds, made primarily from Tempranillo (called Cencibel in this region). Drink at three to four years old. ☆→☆☆

VEGA SICILIA UNICO

 Flagship wine of the Ribera del Duero region released after about ten years ageing and exceptionally long-lived. ☆☆☆

Food and occasions

It is unwise (as well as a waste) to serve up a very old or unusual wine unless you know your guests will enjoy it. You also need to be careful about the kind of food you serve. The delicate flavours of mature wines need complementary rather than competing flavours which are more likely to be found in plainly cooked, classic dishes.

Storing and serving

The older a wine gets, the more carefully you should treat it. Older bottles may throw a sediment. Leave them upright twenty-four hours before serving and don't open them too far in advance. Wines that are full-bodied and still likely to be tannic can benefit from decanting.

ROSE WINES

One of the biggest changes in the wine world over the last few years has been a shift in the fortunes of rosé, which has gone from being a slightly embarrassing girly drink to an almost cultshly popular summer wine. This is partly due to the much improved quality of the rosés available, but also to the more full-bodied style that has been popularized by New World winemakers especially in Australia, California, and Chile.

Rosé is of course made from red wine grapes but produced in a similar style to white wine apart from the fact that the crushed grapes are left in contact long enough with the juice to colour the wine. The style depends on how long the juice remains in contact with the skins. If skin-contact is only brief you will get a pale pink colour and a delicate fruit flavour. When extended, the result is darker and gutsier. But part of the charm of rosés is this variation in colour from the delicate onion-skin, pinky beige colour, through candyfloss pink, to rich, golden salmon and almost reddish magenta.

Versatile summer drinking

Almost all parts of southern Europe produce a simple rosé for everyday drinking. Light, low in alcohol, it is perfect for warm weather. But there are more serious rosés, notably from Provence, the southern Rhône, and Bordeaux. In Provence, wines from appellations such as Bandol and Bellet command prices as high as their red and white counterparts. Tavel, in the southern Rhône has always produced a full-bodied, alcoholic rosé even before this style became fashionable.

More widely available are Bordeaux rosés which provide particularly elegant drinking. And there is more to offer from the Loire than the rather dull sweetish rosés like Rosé d'Anjou. Try Rosé de Loire and Cabernet d'Anjou which are made in a drier, crisper style or the rosés from red wine areas such as Chinon, Bourgueil, and Sancerre.

If you prefer a more robust, rustic style of rosé the best hunting grounds are Spain's *rosados* and the traditional wines of the Languedoc – certainly the wines to drink if you visit the region. And the wines of Costières de Nîmes represent exceptionally good value.

In the New World, most rosés are made from a single grape variety, the most favoured being Grenache, Shiraz, and Cabernet Sauvignon. Like New World reds, they tend to be much richer, sweeter, and fruitier than their European counterparts. They are also much higher in alcohol and lower in acidity.

In California there is a trend towards drier, more full-bodied rosés promoted by a group calling themselves RAP (Rosé Avengers & Producers!) reacting to the dominance of the USA's ever popular medium-dry white Zinfandel.

Elsewhere there is also a decline in medium-dry styles such as Rosé d'Anjou and Mateus Rosé (which has recently launched a drier version), with consumers finding today's ripe fruity rosés more to their taste.

The other popular popular style of rosé is sparkling, most notably rosé Champagne which is regarded as an equal of its non-rosé equivalent. And there are now many attractive rosé sparklers (*see* page 89), which make excellent summer party drinking.

There are certainly signs of producers taking rosé a lot more seriously and giving it the same care and attention they do to their premium red and white wines; and of consumers buying different styles of rosé for different occasions. Its compatibility with modern Asian-influenced food guarantees it year-round popularity. The rosé revolution rolls on!

Label clues

As with other still wines, one of the best clues to the style of a rosé is alcohol content. Lighter rosés will tend to be eleven to twelve degrees, more robust ones up to fourteen or even 14.5 degrees. The colour is also a giveaway. The darker the wine, the more full-bodied and fruity it is likely to be. Since rosé should be drunk as fresh as possible, make sure it comes from a recent vintage.

Above *California is one of the largest producers of rosé ("blush") wines. In this vineyard, the frames help to train the vines in a way that gives the grapes maximum exposure to the sun.*

Far left *Rosé drinking is an integral part of the French way of life in Provence and other parts of southern France, where it is more popular than white wine.*

Starting points	
Dry, crisp, and elegant	**Full-bodied/rustic**
Bordeaux Marsannay	Spanish Rosado Languedoc Rosé Tavel
New World flavours	**Light/Medium-dry**
Cabernet Sauvignon Rosé Grenache Rosé Syrah/Shiraz Rosé	Côtes de Provence Rosé d'Anjou

BERGERAC ROSE

A pretty, strawberry flavoured rosé from the Dordogne region in southwest France, less high profile but produced in a very similar style to BORDEAUX. Worth looking out for. ☆☆

"BLUSH"

A term originated in the late 1980s in California as a brilliant marketing device to resuscitate declining sales of rosé. It is now widely used elsewhere in the world to indicate a light, usually slightly sweetish style of rosé. ☆

BORDEAUX

Rosé production is on the increase in Bordeaux. In fact producers such as Château de Sours and Château Méaume make some of the most elegant rosés on the market, predominantly from MERLOT, rather than the more traditional CABERNET SAUVIGNON. They are bone dry, but full-flavoured with lovely light, soft, raspberry fruit. ☆☆

CABERNET SAUVIGNON

As you might expect, Cabernet Sauvignon makes a dry, crisp, full-bodied style of rosé with a characteristic blackcurrant note to the fruit. It's a popular choice among winemakers in Chile and Eastern Europe. ☆→☆☆

CINSAULT

Cinsault is widely used throughout the LANGUEDOC and PROVENCE for rosé. It is often blended with GRENACHE to make a particularly robust full-bodied style of wine. ☆→☆☆

CLAIRET

Nearer to a light red than a rosé, clairet, which was the origin of the word claret, has been produced in BORDEAUX for years and actually has its own appellation. It is less common than it once was. ☆☆

GRENACHE

One of the most popular varieties for producing full-bodied dry rosés, especially in Spain, Southern France, and Australia. ☆→☆☆

LANGUEDOC ROSE

The consumer drink of choice in the Languedoc, usually made in a dry, crisp, medium-bodied style. There are particularly good producers in Faugères and good value in Costières de Nîmes. ☆→☆☆

LOIRE ROSE

Traditionally one of the least exciting rosés, medium dry, **Rosé d'Anjou**, made from the undistinguished Grolleau grape, is slowly improving. Considerably better are the drier, more elegant **Rosé de Loire** and **Cabernet d'Anjou** which are generally made from Cabernet Franc. **Bourgueil** and **Chinon** also make good rosé, though it is by no means cheap. ☆☆→☆☆☆

MATEUS ROSE

This famous sweetish, slightly fizzy rosé, in its distinctive round bottle, was a common starting point for many wine-drinkers in the 1960s and 1970s. Since then its popularity has declined, but, it's a better drink than many people think. There is now a drier version available. ☆☆

MERLOT

Not a traditional grape variety for rosé, but increasingly popular particularly in Bordeaux for its attractive soft red berry fruit. ☆→☆☆

MOURVEDRE

Exotic southern French variety that is used to make some of the world's more serious rosés including **Bandol**. ☆☆→☆☆☆

PINOT NOIR

Pinot Noir, as you might expect, makes a more delicately fruity style of rosé. Examples are **Marsannay** from Burgundy and **Sancerre Rosé** which has a distinctive pale strawberry red colour. ☆→☆☆☆

PROVENCE AND RHONE ROSE

 Provence is the region most associated with rosé drinking, though its fashionability often means the quality of the wines doesn't quite live up to their price. Most are made from a blend of GRENACHE and CINSAULT, labelled as **Côtes de Provence**, and are rarely more than refreshing light, quaffing wines. More ambitious, stylish wines from small appellations such as **Bandol**, **Cassis,** and **Palette** tend also to include MOURVEDRE. Many red wine-producing regions in the Rhône, including Côtes du Rhône, also make rosé, usually in a more robust style. *See also* TAVEL. ☆☆→☆☆☆

ROSADO – Spain

 Rosé drinking is a way of life for large parts of Spain, particularly in Navarra and Rioja. Most are based on GRENACHE (Garnacha) and have an endearingly robust, rustic quality that works well with tapas and robust seafood dishes. ☆→☆☆

ROSATO

 Rosé or *rosato* as Italians call it hasn't been hugely popular in Italy, but some elegant baby pink rosés are emerging, often blended with popular Pinot Grigio. ☆→☆☆

SYRAH

 A grape variety increasingly favoured (especially among the the new generation of winemakers in the LANGUEDOC) for producing full-flavoured, fruity rosés with a characteristic Syrah spiciness. Also popular in California and Argentina. ☆→☆☆

TAVEL

 This most famous of French rosés (the appellation makes nothing else) comes from the southern Rhône. Predominantly made from GRENACHE it has traditionally been quite full-bodied and alcoholic, and tastes better with food. Some producers are making their wines in a fruitier style. ☆☆→☆☆☆

VIN GRIS

 An ultra pale type of rosé made by leaving the juice in minimum contact with the skins. Less popular than it once was. ☆→☆☆

WHITE ZINFANDEL

 Although it is called white, like other rosés, white Zinfandel is made from the red Zinfandel grape. Light, sweet, and slightly fizzy, it has proved hugely popular with the wine drinking public since it was first launched in California in the late 1980s. There is a growing trend to make it slightly drier. ☆→☆☆

Food and occasions

Tailor-made for summer and particularly outdoor eating. It is the perfect wine to take on a picnic or drink with a barbecue in the garden. It is also very flexible with food. Its naturally high acidity makes it an ideal partner for sharply dressed salads, particularly those made with tomato, and it works well with many Asian cuisines.

Storing and serving

Don't even think about laying rosé down. You should drink it as soon as possible after you've bought it. Treat it like a dry white wine and serve it well chilled.

CHAMPAGNE AND SPARKLING WINE

Most people are not aware of the differences in style among sparkling wines. It's more a question of image. If it's an occasion where we want to make an impression we go for Champagne. If it's less important we are prepared to consider a sparkler.

Such an approach fails to recognize what has been going on over the last few years. A few decades ago the Champagne producers had the quality sparkling wine market to themselves. Now places like California and New Zealand rival them for quality, often, ironically, with the help of those self-same Champagne producers who have seen the opportunity to make fine wines in the New World and set up their own bases there. The New World has also shown a growing self-confidence about making wines that are not in the style of Champagne, wines that are less elegant certainly, but much smoother, fruitier, and easier to drink.

Sparkling wine production is best suited to the cooler wine regions of the world, though few are as cool as Champagne itself. Whereas most winemakers' primary concern is how ripe they can get their grapes, a Champagne or sparkling wine producer is actually looking for a high level of acidity, though in a poor year there is the option of blending in a richer-flavoured wine from previous vintages.

Dark-skinned grape varieties

It may come as a surprise, given that Champagne is a white wine, that two of the grape varieties regularly used in its production are the dark-skinned Pinot Noir and Pinot Meunier. The third is Chardonnay, which can also be used on its own (this is called a Blanc de Blancs). The variations in style between one Champagne and another often reflect the proportions of these grapes the producer uses. More Chardonnay and you get a lighter, more elegant style. More Pinot Noir and you have a Champagne that will be richer and more full-bodied.

Champagne takes time to produce, a complex process of selecting different base wines, blending them, then ageing them in individual bottles for at least eighteen months or more often two to three years. Grapes are also traditionally picked by hand in the region, a process that helps to explain why Champagne and wines made by similar methods are so expensive. Significantly cheaper sparkling wines are generally made in a huge tank and then bottled under pressure. They lack the complexity of Champagne, but the method is perfectly suited to grape varieties like Moscato (Muscat) where a simple fragrance and flavour is what is wanted.

Undoubtedly you pay a premium for the Champagne name, so if you enjoy drinking sparkling wine for its own sake rather than just for a celebration, it's worth exploring outside the region for a style that appeals. In France the main area of sparkling wine production is the Loire though there is also some produced in Alsace, Burgundy, and a small pocket around Limoux in the south of France. The Spanish have their crisp, dry cava, while the Italians have a strong tradition of producing semi-sweet *spumante* wines from the Muscat grape.

But it has been from the New World that the biggest challenge to Champagne has come, particularly where the *champenois* themselves have set up shop. The highest quality is to be found in California and New Zealand, though it is Australia – never afraid to break with convention and do its own thing – that offers the widest choice of prices and styles, including a spectacularly fruity style of red sparkling wine. South Africa, though it doesn't always deliver on quality, can also provide very good full-bodied, rich-tasting wines.

Label clues

It is simple to tell whether a Champagne is non-vintage or vintage. Only vintage Champagne actually gives the year on the label. The other clue to style is the word *"brut"* which indicates that it is made in a dry style. The terms *"sec"* or *"demi-sec"* mean off-dry or medium-sweet.

Above *The necks of Champagne bottles are upended and frozen to remove the yeast that has accumulated during the long ageing process before the bottles are topped up with sweetened wine (dosage).*

Far left *The pastoral countryside of the Champagne region in northeast France – an area whose still wines were generally so harsh that an ingenious method was devised to make them more enjoyable. This is now referred to as the "méthode traditionelle".*

Starting points	
Light and creamy	**Rich and toasty**
Sparkling Chardonnay	Top New Zealand sparkling wine
Crémant de Bourgogne	Top Californian sparkling wine
Blanc de Blancs Champagne	Grand Marque NV Champagne
	Vintage Champagne
Dry, crisp, and yeasty	**Medium-dry**
Cava	Moscato d'Asti
Saumur Brut	Asti
Inexpensive NV Champagne	Demi-Sec Champagne

BLANC DE BLANCS

Literally a white wine made from white grapes, this description indicates that a Champagne has been made from Chardonnay alone. As a result it is likely to be lighter, creamier, and less toasty than one made from a high proportion of Pinot Noir and Pinot Meunier. ☆☆→☆☆☆

BLANC DE NOIRS

Less common than BLANC DE BLANCS this means a Champagne made only from dark-skinned grapes (Pinot Noir and Pinot Meunier) and which is consequently likely to be more full-bodied. It's a style common in the Aube, the area of Champagne to the south of the region which produces some very good value Champagnes. ☆☆→☆☆☆

BRUT

The term used to indicate that a Champagne is dry. Champagnes that receive no "*dosage*" the sweet wine solution that is added to most Champagnes) are sometimes labelled "ultra brut" or "brut nature". ☆→☆☆

DEMI-SEC

Confusingly the term used to describe a sweet Champagne is *demi-sec* (literally half-dry), though in most cases the wine will be sweet enough to drink with a dessert. More recently some producers (including Veuve Clicquot and Roederer) have introduced a category called "**rich**" – which is exactly that: sweeter than normal but luscious and full-bodied. These wines work well with spicy food and with rich dishes like *foie gras*. ☆☆→☆☆☆

GRAND CRU

In Champagne this means that the grapes have come from a vineyard officially designated *grand cru*. However, the wine may not necessarily be of such high quality as a PRESTIGE CUVEE. ☆☆☆

MAGNUM

Champagne that is bottled in a magnum (1.5 litres) generally ages better than a standard sized bottle, resulting in a richer, fuller-tasting style. There is also the element of show. It always seems much more impressive to serve up one large bottle than two small ones – and it generally costs little more. ☆☆→☆☆☆

METHODE TRADITIONELLE

The way Champagne is produced (called the *méthode champenoise* within the Champagne region, méthode traditionelle outside it) also gives the wine its distinctive flavour. Once the winemaker has blended the different individual components of his or her wine (which are drawn from different vineyards and different years), sugar and yeast are added and the resulting wine is actually fermented in the bottle, creating the carbon dioxide that is finally released as bubbles when the cork pops. This fermentation process creates a residue, the lees, which enriches the flavour of the Champagne as it lies in the bottle. The longer the Champagne stays in contact with its lees the better. Less than eighteen months and it won't develop that typical yeasty, biscuity character that makes Champagne so distinctive.

The final step is that the bottle is gradually up-ended (traditionally by hand, increasingly by machine) so that the yeast residues are deposited in the neck of the bottle. Then the neck of the bottle is quickly frozen, the residue discarded and the bottle topped up with a sweetened wine (called the *dosage*) which is adjusted depending on how sweet the winemaker wants the final wine to be.

NON-VINTAGE

The term non-vintage (NV) has negative connotations, implying that it's second best to VINTAGE Champagne. But, in fact, it refers more to the way the Champagne is made, blending wine from different vintages in order to achieve a consistent style. Nevertheless, a non-vintage Champagne is likely to contain a higher proportion of young wine and so the style is likely to be dry, fresh, and crisp, with a more or less yeasty, toasty or honeyed character depending on how long it has been left on its lees (*see* above).

Most of the well-known brands, or **Grandes Marques** as they are known in Champagne, will have been aged for two to three years, though the minimum requirement is only twelve months. So there is a world of difference in style between a cut-price Champagne which may taste quite thin and acidic and the non-vintage Champagne of a Grande Marque like Bollinger or a highly regarded independent producer such as Billecart-Salmon. There are also Champagne producers who cultivate a distinctive house style. Taittinger, for example, uses a high proportion of Chardonnay to produce a particularly light, elegant style of Champagne. Veuve Clicquot is richer and more full-bodied. ☆→☆☆

RECEMMENT DEGORGE

 This term means a mature wine that has been recently bottled giving it a particularly fresh, elegant flavour. Only the house of Bollinger has the right to use the initials RD as an abbreviation (the house has registered "RD" as a trademark). ☆☆☆

RECOLTANT-MANIPULANT

You can tell if a wine is a grower's Champagne by the initials RM (récoltant-manipulant) on the label. Although the French like to buy their Champagne direct from their favourite grower, it's a rather more hazardous enterprise if you live outside the country. As a small grower hasn't got the same range of grapes or reserves of old wine to call on as the big Champagne houses, quality can fluctuate from one year to another, but the best can offer better value than the big brands. ☆→☆☆

ROSE

 Rosé Champagne is taken very seriously in the region, with several houses actually producing vintage versions. Some are produced like other rosés by leaving the juice

in contact with dark-coloured grape skins, others by adding a little red wine to the blend before the second fermentation takes place. ☆→☆☆☆

PRESTIGE CUVEE

 A term used by Champagne producers to describe their best VINTAGE Champagnes. Well known examples are Dom Pérignon, Roederer Cristal, Veuve Cliquot La Grande Dame, and Bollinger RD. ☆☆☆

VINTAGE

 Vintage Champagne comes from a single, exceptional year (most recently 1996, 1995, and 2002). It should in theory be richer, toastier, and generally more full-flavoured than a NON-VINTAGE Champagne. But that isn't a taste that necessarily appeals to all wine-drinkers, some of whom may actually prefer a fresher style. Over time (and it will last for several years) it can acquire quite a mature vinous character particularly if, like Krug, it is aged in oak. ☆☆→☆☆☆

ASTI

 In spite of the fact that it has been renamed Asti, Asti Spumante is still the name by which many people know this best-selling medium-dry wine. On these grounds alone it tends to be looked down on, although drunk in the right context (on a warm summer's day), the refreshingly grapey end result can be more enjoyable than wine snobs admit. It's also low in alcohol (about seven per cent ABV). ☆

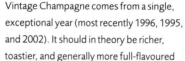

Food and occasions

Although you may still feel that you should serve Champagne for a celebration these days you don't have to. What's more important is to tailor the style of wine to the occasion. If it's a stand-up party or reception with canapés or finger food, go for a lighter wine. If it's a special dinner where you will be drinking sparkling wine throughout the meal go for a richer, fuller-flavoured style. In fact, Champagne and other sparkling wines are surprisingly flexible with food. The only combinations that can be tricky are dry Champagne with a rich dessert that emphasizes its acidity and hot spicy dishes (though both Chinese and Japanese food can work well). Sweeter sparklers like Demi-Sec Champagne and Asti can be delicious with fruit-based desserts and cakes, while red sparklers are an adventurous choice for a barbecue.

AUSTRALIA

Given its warmer than average climate, it is not surprising that many Australian sparkling wines are more obviously fruity and less acidic than their European counterparts. Most provide uncomplicated, good value drinking. But there are a handful of producers, such as Domaine Chandon and Jansz and Pirie in Tasmania, who are producing more ambitiously elegant wines. ☆→☆☆

BLANQUETTE & CREMANT DE LIMOUX

This soft, creamy, slightly appley sparkler from the Languedoc reputedly pre-dates Champagne. It is made primarily from the local Mauzac grape together with some Chenin Blanc and CHARDONNAY. Recently more wines are being marketed as Crémant de Limoux, which permits a higher amount of Chardonnay, and have a creaminess more to the modern taste. ☆→☆☆

CALIFORNIA

Along with New Zealand, California produces some of the best quality sparkling wine outside Champagne thanks to past investment from Champagne houses including Moët & Chandon (Domaine Chandon) and Mumm (Mumm Cuvée Napa). Some, like Mumm, are made in a lighter, vanilla-scented style; others, like Roederer Estate's, are richer and more toasty. ☆☆

CAP CLASSIQUE

This is the term used in South Africa to describe sparkling wines made by the traditional Champagne method, some of the best of which come from the Franschhoek region. They tend to be more classic in style than similarly priced Australian sparklers, though most lack the finess of the best wines from New Zealand and California. ☆☆

CAVA

Cava, which comes from Spain, is the great sparkling wine success story of recent years, producing consistently drinkable dry, yeasty sparkling wine at an exceptionally reasonable price. Vintage cavas are more full-bodied and complex. ☆→☆☆

CHARDONNAY

The most popular grape for New World sparkling wines, with more of a creamy vanilla soda flavour than the tropical fruit character associated with this grape. ☆→☆☆

CLAIRETTE DE DIE

A little-known delicately sweet French sparkling wine from the Rhône Valley. There is also a **Crémant de Die** which is similar in style. ☆

CREMANT DE BOURGOGNE

With the same grapes as Champagne (CHARDONNAY and Pinot Noir) and only a slightly warmer climate, Burgundy seems a natural area to make *crémant* – the word the French use outside Champagne for sparkling wine. And although in no way as fine or as complex, it can be very good. Other *crémants* to look for include **Crémant d'Alsace** and **Crémant de Loire**. ☆☆

ENGLAND

The similarity between soils in southeast England and the Champagne region of France accounts for the high quality of English sparkling wines, especially from award-winning producers Nyetimber and RidgeView. ☆☆→☆☆☆

MOSCATO D'ASTI

This softly sparkling off-dry wine is similar in style and produced in the same region (the northwest of Italy) as ASTI but tends to be of better quality. ☆

NEW ZEALAND

The other major New World contender for Champagne's crown. Ideal cool growing conditions result in sophisticated sparkling wines, helped, in the case of top producers such as Deutz and Cloudy Bay's Pelorus, by input from Champagne. The less expensive but still richly flavoured Lindauer range also offers great value. ☆☆→☆☆☆

PROSECCO

 Much improved and fashionable soft Italian sparkling wine made in the Veneto from the Prosecco grape variety. It is also the base of the traditional Bellini cocktail. ☆☆→☆☆☆

ROSE

  A number of the regions which produce sparkling wine also produce a rosé version – **Cava Rosado** is an example. But the country that has really gone for sparkling rosé in a big way is Australia, with attractive soft strawberry flavoured sparklers like Jacob's Creek sparkling rosé. ☆→☆☆☆

SAUMUR BRUT

 A traditional method sparkling wine made predominantly from Chenin Blanc. Slightly sharp for modern tastes. ☆☆

SEKT

 Sekt is the German word for sparkling wine, although much of the wine that goes into the large commercial brands is produced outside Germany itself. (If the grapes do originate in Germany it will be labelled "Deutscher Sekt" and is likely to be of better quality.) "*Trocken*" is the indication that it it is dry – and it can in fact be quite sharp. "*Halbtrocken*" (literally "half dry") versions also exist. ☆→☆☆

SHIRAZ & OTHER SPARKLING REDS

 Australia is in the vanguard of red sparkling wine production with exuberantly fruity wines like **Sparkling Shiraz**, **Sparkling Cabernet**, and **Sparkling Grenache** that are perfect for barbecues and the Christmas turkey. By and large this is not a style favoured in Europe with the notable exception of **Lambrusco**. The authentic version of which has a refreshingly bitter cherry flavour. A few red sparkling wines are also made in the Loire. ☆☆→☆☆☆

VEUVE DU VERNAY

 Rather dull commercial French sparkler which has been overtaken in the quality and value-for-money stakes by its competitors. ☆☆

VOUVRAY MOUSSEUX

 A softly honeyed, sparkling version of Vouvray generally a cut above the other Chenin Blanc sparklers of the Loire. If you want a dry wine, make sure it isn't one of the *demi-sec* versions which are also available. ☆☆

Storing and serving

It is not worth laying down New World or non-vintage Champagne for any length of time, although most Champagnes can benefit from a six month rest before you pop the cork. Vintage Champagnes will last a good deal longer: from three to five years for basic vintage Champagnes (depending, of course, on how long they've been stored by the time you buy them), to a good decade in the case of prestige cuvées. A bigger bottle will last longer than a smaller one. It is important to chill Champagne and sparkling wine well before serving – it not only tastes better, it makes it safer to open the bottle.

SWEET WINES

It is a shame that drinking sweet wines has become such an unfamiliar experience for many, as they represent some of the most luscious and complex flavours in the wine world. However, the combination of their sheer sweetness and alcoholic strength undoubtedly makes them wines for special occasions rather than everyday drinking.

Historically, sweet wines were more highly regarded than dry. The wine drunk by the Greeks and the Romans was intensely sweet, often infused with herbs or spices. In a hot climate it was the only kind of wine stable enough to survive. The effect of noble rot (the fungus that causes grapes to shrivel, concentrating their juice to a wonderful intensity) was probably recognized as far back as Roman times and certainly in the seventeenth century, when the great Hungarian wine Tokaj was first produced.

Noble rot

Traditionally, the great areas for dessert wines have been where noble rot readily occurs: Bordeaux and the Loire Valley in France, and parts of Germany, Austria, and Hungary. The rot or "botrytis" thrives in certain autumnal weather conditions – cool misty mornings and warm afternoons. The high risk strategy of leaving the grapes on the vine long enough to be affected by botrytis, then painstakingly harvesting the affected berries helps to explain the stratospheric prices of wines like Sauternes. But the wonderfully liquorous texture and uniquely rich, honeyed flavour of these wines is a benchmark for all dessert wines.

There are other methods of making sweet wines. Grapes may be hung up or laid out to dry – as favoured in Greece and Italy; the wine's eventual strength and concentration depends on how dessicated they get. Another method, popular for Muscat (*see* entry), is to add alcohol before the fermentation process is complete, creating a strong, sweet wine which retains its floral, aromatic character; this type of wine is called *vin doux naturel*. Some wines are made dry, and have sweet grape juice added, while others have their sweetness boosted with sugar.

Muscat, with its aromatic, floral character, is the grape variety most associated with dessert wines, but other light-skinned grape varieties are also used extensively. The two stars are Riesling and Semillon, both particularly susceptible to noble rot, but some fine wines are also made from Chenin (in the Loire) and Gewurztraminer (Alsace).

With so many different styles, sweet wines are confusing, but the easiest way to get a grip on them is by colour and price. The lighter the colour, the fresher the style tends to be. A pale straw coloured wine will generally taste lighter and fresher than a rich apricot coloured one.

Inexpensive wines, including most Muscats, tend to be less sweet than more expensively produced botrytized wines like Sauternes or intensely concentrated wines like Eiswein or Trockenbeerenauslese which are so sweet they can only be sipped in tiny amounts. Check the sweetness rating (one to five) alongside each entry.

Many expensive dessert wines need ageing to counterbalance their initial sweetness. German Rieslings in particular can be unbearably sweet to begin with, only starting to show a graceful balance after several years in the bottle. Chenin – the basis of the famous Loire dessert wines like Vouvray and Bonnezeaux can go through a "dumb" period, when they really are quite dull, before emerging in all their honeyed majesty. Like aged reds, the taste of mature sweet wine may not immediately appeal, but they are worth persevering with.

The big advantage of dessert wines is that you can buy most of them in half bottles. And for a dinner party that's all you need to give your guests a really rather special treat.

Label Clues

Look out for words that indicate the wine is sweet: botrytis or botrytized, late harvest, late-picked, Vendange Tardive, *moelleux*, *liquoreux*, *doux* and *dulce*. Alcohol content is slightly less important than it is for other wines. A southern French Muscat of fifteen degrees for instance may not taste as sweet as a German Beerenauslese of seven or eight degrees.

Above *Grapes affected by the revolting looking rot called "botrytis" (or noble rot) produce the most luscious, honeyed wines that can age for decades.*

Far left *Warm autumn mists rising from the Ciron stream running through Sauternes and Barsac encourage the growth of "botrytis" which makes these wines so special.*

Starting points	
Light	**Rich**
Moscatel de Valencia	Muscat de Beaumes de Venise
Premières Côtes de Bordeaux	Late Harvest Riesling or Semillon
Coteaux du Layon	Tokaj
Sauternes	Vin Santo
Intensely sweet	**Sweet Red Wines**
Beerenauslese	Mavrodaphne of Patras
Trockenbeerenauslese	South African Muscadel
Eiswein	Recioto della Valpolicella

AUSBRUCH

 An Austrian wine classification indicating an intensely concentrated sweet wine made from BOTRYTIS-affected grapes – an Austrian equivalent to SAUTERNES. Most is produced around the town of Rust. ☆☆→☆☆☆

AUSLESE

 Auslese is the recognized German wine category for grapes that are selected for being particularly ripe. It is generally sweet (though there are some dry versions), but not as sweet as BEERENAUSLESE. Quality varies considerably from the slightly sickly, commercial Auslesen, to very fine, concentrated, elegant RIESLINGS from individual growers. A similar classification is used in Austria. ☆→☆☆☆

BARSAC

 The name of the most celebrated individual village in SAUTERNES which has its own appellation but may call its wines Barsac-Sauternes. The wines are virtually indistinguishable from those of Sauternes and the appellation includes many of Bordeaux's best properties, most notably **Château Climens**. ☆☆→☆☆☆

BEERENAUSLESE

 The next grade of sweetness up from AUSLESE involving even riper grapes, usually those affected by BOTRYTIS. The resulting wine is intensely sweet, though generally balanced by a high level of acidity. ☆☆→☆☆☆

BONNEZEAUX

 One of the two great sweet wines of the Loire from the COTEAUX DU LAYON area, the other being **Quarts de Chaume**. These are made from Chenin Blanc and are not at their best for at least ten years and may last at least a couple of decades longer than that. ☆☆☆

BOTRYTIS/BOTRYTIZED

 A description used on labels to indicate that the wine is made from grapes affected by noble rot (*see* previous pages). In the New World this is quite likely to have been induced artifically. ☆☆→☆☆☆

COTEAUX DU LAYON

 A large appellation in Anjou in the Loire Valley producing a wide range of wines from Chenin, from simple honeyed, medium-dry whites, to richer, complex wines from individual villages such as **Chaume** and **Rablay sur Layon**. ☆☆→☆☆☆

EISWEIN

 The most intensely sweet of all dessert wines made from frozen grapes which are picked as late as January. It is a particular speciality of northern Germany, though there is also some made in Austria, and it is increasingly popular in Canada and Washington State where it is called **Icewine**. Because of the very low yields – and its fashionability, particularly among Far Eastern buyers – it commands very high prices. ☆☆☆

GEWURZTRAMINER

 A grape variety well suited to dessert wine production, particularly in Alsace which has established a reputation for powerful, rich, aromatic VENDANGE TARDIVE and SELECTION DES GRAINS NOBLES wines. They can lose their distinctive aromatic quality over time. ☆☆☆

GRAVES SUPERIEURES

 A less well-known Bordeaux appellation that can produce some decent basic sweet wines, but which only hint at the opulence of neighbouring SAUTERNES and BARSAC. ☆

JURANCON

 An exotically flavoured, fruity dessert wine from the southwest of France, near the Spanish border, made from local grape varieties, principally Petit Manseng. (Dry versions are labelled Jurançon Sec). ☆☆→☆☆☆

LATE HARVEST/LATE-PICKED

 The anglicized version of VENDANGE TARDIVE; a term used predominantly in the New World to indicate a sweet wine made from super-ripe grapes. ☆→☆☆

MAVRODAPHNE OF PATRAS

 An exotic, rich, almost port-like red Greek dessert wine. Unbelievabley cheap and one of the best wine matches for chocolate. ☆

MONBAZILLAC

(2) Attractive citrussy SEMILLON/Sauvignon-based wine from the Bergerac region in the southwest of France made in a similar style, though not always attaining the same quality, as sweet Bordeaux. Neighbouring Saussignac is made in a similar style. ☆☆

MONTLOUIS

(3) A neighbouring appellation to VOUVRAY, but much less well-known sweet (*moelleux*). Montlouis wines have a similar honeyed style, but not are always as distinguished. A limited amount of botrytized dessert wine is also produced in exceptional years in nearby appellation of **Jasnières**. ☆☆☆

MOSCATEL DE VALENCIA

(2) A light, refreshingly grapey Spanish MUSCAT that represents exceptionally good value for money. It generally comes in a distinctive frosted flute-shaped bottle. ☆☆

MOSCATO PASSITO DI PANTELLERIA

(3) An intense, rich, golden, almost apricot-like MUSCAT, from the island of Pantelleria off Sicily, made by the *passito* method from grapes laid out to dry until they resemble raisins. ☆☆

MUSCADEL

(3) A dark-berried South African strain of MUSCAT, traditionally used for the famous South African fortified wine **Constantia**. Also used to make a rich, sweet, port-like dessert wine. ☆

MUSCAT, MOSCATO, MOSCATEL

(1-3) The Muscat grape is used all over the wine world to make an astonishingly diverse range of wines, from the fresh, grapey **Moscatel de Valencia**, to the intensely rich, toffeed **Liqueur Muscats** of the Rutherglen region in Australia. Confusingly, there are more than 200 different varieties of Muscat, but the most widely planted are Muscat Blanc à Petits Grains and Muscat d'Alexandrie which go under a number of different synonyms. Most are in fact a *vin doux naturel* (*see* pages 92–3). Although this technically brings them into the fortified category, most Muscats are regarded primarily as a dessert wine, rather than one to sip at the end of a meal like port. In fact, Muscats, like those from Frontignan and Beaumes-de-Venise (*see* below), are frequently served as an apéritif in France. Richer, heavier styles like Australian Liqueur Muscats are dealt with in the next section and sparkling wines made from Muscat (Moscato) on page 90. ☆→☆☆

MUSCAT D'ALSACE

(2) Muscat is usually produced as a dry wine in Alsace but some winemakers do produce VENDANGE TARDIVE (late-picked) versions. Both are usually elegant and expensive. ☆☆☆

MUSCAT DE BEAUMES-DE-VENISE

(3) Less fashionable than it once was but still one of the very best known Muscats on the

Food and occasions

While sweet wines are the obvious choice to accompany a dessert, you can also drink them, as the French do, as an apéritif. The general rule with a dessert is that the wine should be sweeter than the pudding. Lighter wines such as Muscats and sweet Bordeaux are best with simple fruit flavours, particularly apple-, pear- or peach-based desserts (red fruits can be tricky unless they are offset by cream). For richer puddings, such as those made from chocolate, look to more robust wines such as Australian Liqueur Muscats or even sweet red wines.

market, this luscious sweet wine from the southern end of the Rhône Valley is one of the easiest ways into dessert wine drinking. ☆☆

MUSCAT DE FRONTIGNAN

(3) Originally the most important of the southern French Muscats that are produced in the Languedoc, Frontignan – as it is now called – is made in a much lighter style than than the dark, rich, raisiny wines that used to predominate in the region. Other similarly styled Languedoc Muscats are **Muscat de Lunel**, **Muscat de Mireval**, **Muscat de Rivesaltes**, and **Muscat St-Jean-de-Minervois**. ☆

ORANGE MUSCAT

(3) A distinctive style of MUSCAT that has been enterprizingly promoted by Andrew Quady in California and Brown Brothers in Australia: rich and liquorous with a pronounced orange peel aroma and flavour. ☆☆→☆☆☆

PACHERENC DU VIC-BILH – *Moelleux*

(2) A rare but highly regarded dessert wine produced in the foothills of the Pyrenees in southwest France. Pacherenc du Vic-Bilh is made in a similar style to JURANCON which comes from nearby. ☆☆→☆☆☆

PREMIERES COTES DE BORDEAUX

(2) A large area on the Right Bank of the Garonne, which now produces more dry white, rosé, and red wines than it does dessert wines. Basic sweet Premières Côtes de Bordeaux is rarely distinguished, but some fine SAUTERNES-style wines are produced in individual villages such as **Cadillac**, **Loupiac**, and **Ste-Croix-du-Mont**. ☆☆

RECIOTO DELLA VALPOLICELLA

(3) This obscure sweet red dessert wine is made from the same grape varieties as Valpolicella (*see* page 65), but left out to dry for several months on straw mats. **Recioto di Soave**, which is rarer still, is made in a similar fashion, though from light-skinned grapes. ☆☆

RIESLING

(2) Riesling is the grape variety used in Germany's finest dessert wines. Its refreshing acidity proves to be a perfect counterfoil to what can be quite intense levels of sweetness. It is also popular in Alsace, Austria, and Australia, where it is used to make BOTRYTIZED or LATE HARVEST wines. ☆☆→☆☆☆

SAMOS

(3) Greek island famous for its excellent and unbelievabley inexpensive Muscats. Look out for ones labelled "Nectar". ☆☆→☆☆☆

SAUTERNES

(3) One of the few areas to have the ideal conditions for the cultivation of noble rot, Sauternes wines are justly regarded as some of the finest in the world. Made principally from SEMILLON with a small amount of Sauvignon and Muscadelle. When young it has a light, luscious honey and citrus character which ages gracefully over time to a richer, nuttier flavour of dried apricots, figs, and toasted hazelnuts. Higher quality wines are named after the five major villages in the region, the most famous of which is BARSAC. The most celebrated individual property is **Château d'Yquem**, whose better vintages can last for more than a century. ☆☆→☆☆☆

SELECTION DES GRAINS NOBLES

(4) The sweetest and most expensive of Alsace wines achieved by hand-selecting ultra ripe often BOTRYTIZED grapes from MUSCAT, Pinot Gris, RIESLING or GEWURZTRAMINER vines. ☆☆☆

SEMILLON

(3) The backbone of SAUTERNES and the other sweet wines of Bordeaux and Bergerac, the Semillon grape's thin skin makes it ideal for sweet winemaking because of its susceptibility to noble rot. It is also widely used in Australia to make LATE HARVEST and BOTRYTIZED wines. ☆☆

TOKAJ

(3-5) Hungarian Tokaj is undoubtedly one of the world's great classic dessert wines, having been produced there for over three centuries. The most widely available style is **Tokaj Aszú**,

a sumptuously rich, golden wine brimming with luscious dried fig, raisin, and apricot flavours. It is officially graded by the number of "puttonyos" it contains (barrels of sweet grape pulp that are added to the wine before the secondary fermentation, three "putts" being the least sweet and six the sweetest). The rarest kind of Tokaj is **Essencia** which is made from the minute amounts of juice that ooze out of the BOTRYTIZED grapes.
☆☆→☆☆☆

TROCKENBEERENAUSLESE

Trockenbeerenauslese (or TBA as it is known for short) is principally a German dessert wine that is made only in exceptional years from hand-picked BOTRYTIZED grapes. The result is an intensely liquorous sweet wine, but with a piercing acidity which prevents it from being cloying. Ideal conditions for making TBA also occur in the Burgenland region of Austria where producers such as Alois Kracher and Willi Poitz make spectacularly good wines.
☆☆☆

VENDANGE TARDIVE

A term used principally in Alsace to indicate that a wine has been made from LATE-PICKED grapes. It is normally an indication of sweetness. ☆☆→☆☆☆

VIN DE PAILLE

A rare speciality of the Jura region of France made from grapes that are laid out to dry on straw mats (*pailles*). The

resulting wine is intensely sweet. "Straw wine" is also made in Germany where it is called **Strohwein** and Austria (**Schilfwein**), though these tend to be rather lighter in style. ☆☆☆

VIN SANTO

Over the past few years *vin santo*, along with other Tuscan wines, has become extremely fashionable and consequently expensive. Made from grapes that are either hung or laid out to dry then aged in barrels for anything up to six to eight years, it produces a glorious, golden, nutty wine, which is traditionally served at the end of meal with dipping biscuits (*cantuccini*). It is also made in Umbria and the Trentino. ☆☆→☆☆☆

VISANTO

An exotically dark, delicious wine made on the island of Santorini from the local Assyrtiko grape. ☆☆

VOUVRAY MOELLEUX

As well as producing dry and medium-dry (*demi-sec*) wines, Vouvray, which is made from Chenin Blanc, also produces some of the finest sweet wines in the Loire. They are labelled *moelleux* or, in the case of the very sweetest, **Liquoreux**. Sweet and honeyed when young, they can still taste extraordinarily fresh and fruity after several decades. ☆☆→☆☆☆

Storing and serving

Most inexpensive dessert wines, particularly Muscats, benefit from being drunk quite young so that you get the full benefit of their fresh, grapey flavour. But many dessert wines particularly those from Bordeaux and the Loire have the capacity to age for much longer. Most dessert wines benefit from being well chilled – serve them in small rather than full-sized wine glasses. Once opened they will keep fresh for much longer than dry wines, certainly for a week, and in the case of Tokaj or vin santo, for a good month or more.

FORTIFIED WINES: SHERRY

After years of being regarded as desperately unfashionable, sherry has become cool to drink again thanks to the popularity of tapas bars and Spanish influenced cuisine. Deservedly so. They remain some of the finest wines the world has to offer and their price scarcely reflects the care, time, and effort that goes into their production.

Like port and madeira, sherry is a fortified wine, which means that spirit is added to boose its strength (see below). Most are fortified to 17.5 degrees, though the trend, with fino and manzanilla, is to bottle them at around fifteen per cent.

Spanish style sherry

The sherry Spain produces for export is very different to the sherry the Spanish drink themselves. Many drinkers in the UK still see it as a rather sweet, sticky, fortified wine. The real thing is deliciously tangy and in the main bone dry and well worth getting to know.

Sherry can only be made in a tiny triangle of southern Spain bordered by the towns of Sanlúcar de Barrameda, Puerto de Santa María, and Jerez de la Frontera – the town sherry is named after. Its intensely hot, dry climate and distinctive chalky soil is ideally suited for the production of this uniquely dry, yet full-flavoured style of wine.

The two main types of sherry are fino and oloroso – both made from the local Palomino grape, but subsequently treated very differently. Fino, the lighter style, is fortified to about fifteen degrees, then transferred to oak barrels where it develops and then matures under a thick layer of yeast called *flor*. It is the *flor* that gives the distinctive pale colour and dry, tangy character. Oloroso is fortified to a higher eighteen degrees, too strong for *flor* to develop, and makes a much richer, darker wine.

What gives sherry its distinctive character is the *solera* system, in which wine of differing vintages is kept in rows of barrels, stacked one on top of the other. As the wine from the lower barrels is drawn off for bottling, it is topped up with younger wine from the barrels above, ensuring there is always a freshness to the wine to match its depth and complexity. In the case of fino, the final wine is then fortified again to between fifteen and seventeen degrees. The whole process can take at least four or five years (to be called sherry it has to be matured for at least three). Recently the authorities have allowed producers to indicate the age of sherries that are twelve and fifteen years old on labels and introduce two categories for very old sherries. VORS (very old rare sherry) for ones that are at least thirty years old and VOS for ones of at least twenty years.

Light and dry
FINO

A very light, crisp, dry style of sherry which gets its characteristically tangy taste from the thick layer of yeast (*flor*) under which the wine ages. The Spanish version will be bone dry – piercingly so in the case of a wine like Tio Pepe. Finos produced purely for the export market tend to be smoother and sweeter. ☆→☆☆

MANZANILLA

Generally even drier than FINO, manzanilla is produced in the coastal town of Sanlúcar which gives it its characteristic, almost salty tang. Manzanilla Pasada is a mature manzanilla with a richer nuttier flavour. ☆→☆☆

Light and sweet
PALE CREAM SHERRY

A light, smooth, FINO sherry, sweetened to satisfy the tastes of the export market. ☆

Rich and dry
AMONTILLADO SECO

This is, in fact, FINO sherry, matured beyond the *flor* stage until it develops a dark golden colour and a delicious dry, nutty, toffee flavour. ☆☆→☆☆☆

OLOROSO SECO

Darker and more intense than AMONTILLADO with a rich, raisiny, figgy flavour. ☆☆→☆☆☆

PALO CORTADO

Another authentic Spanish style sherry, nutty and slightly richer than a dry AMONTILLADO, but not quite as rich and concentrated as an OLOROSO. ☆☆→☆☆☆

Rich and sweet
MEDIUM-DRY AMONTILLADO

Although described as "medium-dry" by Spanish standards, this style of wine is quite sweet. ☆

OLOROSO DULCE

Sweet oloroso is one of most glorious after-dinner wines around: a dark, sumptuously sweet wine, almost like liquid Christmas pudding. ☆☆→☆☆☆

RICH CREAM SHERRY

The British style version of an OLOROSO DULCE: equally sweet, but without the balancing acidity and depth of flavour. ☆

PEDRO XIMENEZ (PX)

An extraordinarily intense, dark, treacly sherry used to make OLOROSO DULCE and to sweeten other sherries, but also bottled on its own. Almost too sweet to drink, it makes a sensational topping for vanilla ice cream. ☆☆

MONTILLA and other sherry-style wines

A number of wines are made in a similar style to sherry, including Montilla and other fortified wines from the UK, Cyprus, and South Africa – none of which have sherry's distinction. Exceptions are **Cape White Jerepigo**, a South African wine similar to a dry AMONTILLADO and the FINO-like **Vin Jaune** which comes from the Jura region of France. ☆→☆☆☆

Food and occasions

Fino or dry amontillado make a perfect apéritif. Fino is a partner for Spanish tapas but also goes well with spicy food and all kinds of seafood. Richer sherries, like dry and sweet oloroso, are a good alternative to port with cheese or as an after-dinner drink.

Storing and serving

Fino and manzanilla should be served chilled and as fresh as possible (ideally within forty-eight hours of opening the bottle so it makes good sense to buy them by the half bottle). Other sherries should be served at cool room temperature, but should still be consumed within a few weeks of opening. Neither type of sherry should be decanted. If you drink sherry regularly it's worth investing in a set of tulip shaped copita glasses rather than the traditional schooner which tends to subdue the flavours and aromas of the wine.

FORTIFIED WINES: PORT

Sweet, spicy port is one of the most comforting drinks in the world: a classic end to a Christmas meal, a warming winter nightcap or even the kind of drink to sip as you curl up with a good book.

First made in Portugal in the seventeenth century in response to the demand for a wine that could survive the journey back to England, much about port is still deeply traditional, from the way it is harvested on the vertiginous slopes of the Douro Valley to the arcane serving rituals which still survive in gentlemen's clubs. But the region is modernizing fast. Robotic *lagares* have replaced the traditional foot treading and ports are being released younger, with more vibrant soft fruit, and packaged in contemporary-looking bottles.

Port is made from a wide variety of indigenous Portuguese grapes of which the most widely used are Touriga Nacional, Touriga Francesca, Tinta Barroca, Tinta Cão, and Tinta Roriz. The basic process is simply a question of adding brandy to the partially fermented wine, leaving it with a high degree of sweetness. It is then aged in oak casks for a period before it is either blended with other older or younger wines or bottled as a port from a single vintage. Ports of exceptional quality are bottled early and left to mature in bottle, a slower and more gradual process than ageing them in cask.

The most obvious difference in style is between ruby and tawny port and it's very much a question of personal taste as to whether you like the warming, winter punch-type taste of a Late Bottled Vintage or the drier, nuttier more sherry-like taste of a tawny.

Equally significant is the age of the port – and port is a drink that lasts a very long time. There's more of a difference between a young, fresh, ruby port and a mature vintage port than there is between a basic ruby and a tawny. You may in fact prefer the taste of the younger wine.

Port-style wines

Australia is the country that ostensibly models its fortified wines most closely on port, marketing them as tawny or aged tawny but, in fact, they are sweeter and a lot more fudgy than authentic aged tawny ports – more like an Australian Liqueur Muscat. Some port-style fortified wines are also produced in California and South Africa, but the wines that are most similar in taste to port are the fortified wines of the Roussillon: Banyuls, Maury, and Rivesaltes (*see* Fortified Wines: Madeira and others).

RUBY PORT

A blend of different wines bottled after two to three years' storage in cask, concrete or even stainless steel. Simple, sweet, and brambly. ☆

VINTAGE CHARACTER

Easy to confuse with vintage port but often only a marginal step up in quality from basic RUBY PORT. ☆

LATE BOTTLED VINTAGE (LBV)

Late Bottled Vintage is port from a single vintage that has been matured in cask for four to six years. Generally it is then released for immediate drinking, though some producers mature their wines further in the bottle like a VINTAGE PORT. LBV is much richer and more complex than basic RUBY PORT, with a warming spiciness. ☆☆

VINTAGE PORT

Port producers only "declare" a vintage in what they consider to be an exceptional harvest or when they haven't declared one for a while. Unlike other ports, vintage ports are bottled after two years, but are then allowed to carry on maturing in the bottle for at least another ten to twenty years, during which time they accumulate a heavy sediment. The resulting wine, which needs to be decanted, is richly flavoured, complex, and mellow with deep plum, raisin, and chocolate flavours. ☆☆☆

CRUSTED PORT

Similar to a VINTAGE PORT, but the produce of more than one year. It is bottled a little later, then allowed to mature for a further three or four years in the bottle. This makes for a slightly lighter style of wine. ☆☆

TAWNY PORT

Basic tawny port is generally made from inferior quality wine to ruby port, blended with WHITE PORT to give it its distinctive pale colour. It has little of the depth or nutty character of an aged tawny port. ☆

10-YEAR-OLD TAWNY

The most popular style of tawny has a rich, nutty, toffeed character that comes from an average of ten years' cask-ageing. ☆☆

20, 30, AND 40-YEAR-OLD TAWNIES

As TAWNY PORTS age, they develop a rich, creamy, nutty, intensely elegant style. Thirty- and forty-year-old tawnies are very rare and have a particularly pronounced toasty, nutty character, verging towards complete dryness. ☆☆☆

COLHEITA

This is a TAWNY PORT from a single vintage which has been matured for at least seven years in cask. A more individual and characterful style of port than the standard TEN-YEAR-OLD TAWNY. ☆☆

SINGLE QUINTA

A high quality port made on a single estate or *quinta* in years when there isn't a vintage declaration. It is released after about ten years and is a little lighter than VINTAGE PORT but significantly cheaper. ☆☆

WHITE PORT

Widely drunk in Portugal as a summer drink with tonic, most white port is made in medium-dry style, similar to a pale cream sherry, though there are drier versions that have a crisper, nuttier flavour. ☆

Food and occasions

Too often port is served at the end of an already long and heavy meal, but it makes a better accompaniment to a small snack like cheese and crackers or a piece of cake. Aged tawny ports can make a stylish apéritif.

Storing and serving

It is a myth that all ports need to be decanted. The ones that do are those that accumulate a heavy sediment like vintage port, crusted ports, and single-quinta ports. The other myth about port is that once opened it will keep indefinitely. In fact, you should drink it within a month. The big danger, with vintage port in particular, is opening it up before it's ready. You shouldn't even think about it until it is at least ten years old. Although most port is best served at room temperature, tawny port can be delicious lightly chilled.

FORTIFIED WINES: MADEIRA AND OTHERS

Though treated as a bit of a music hall joke, madeira is undoubtedly up among the greats of the fortified wine world. Its finest wines have the capacity to last not only for decades, but for centuries.

This style of wine developed accidentally as a result of madeira being discovered to improve during long, hot voyages across the equator. These days a similar effect is achieved by warming up the wine in large concrete tanks or in a heated room (*canteiro*), though better quality madeira is aged more slowly in oak casks at a temperature of about 25 °C (77 °F). Some wines involve a combination of the two methods.

Madeira is made in four principal styles, named after the grape varieties from which they are made. The common characteristic is high acidity. **Sercial** is the driest – light, tangy, and crisp with a faint, honeyed flavour offset by a characteristic acidity. It is generally fuller in flavour than a fino sherry, though it develops a drier, more almondy flavour with age. Like fino it can be drunk lightly chilled as an apéritif. **Verdelho** is fuller-flavoured and nuttier, more like an amontillado sherry. It can also be made in a medium-bodied but slightly lighter, less dry style.

Bual is distinctly sweet but full-bodied, nutty, and raisiny, with a fragrant, almost smoky character. It can be good with cheese instead of a tawny port. **Malmsey** is the sweetest of the madeira styles and is in fact made from the Malvasia grape variety, whose name got corrupted to malmsey. It is intensely rich with a dark treacle-toffee colour and flavour-like a sticky and well-matured fruit cake, but because of its high level of acidity it isn't remotely cloying. It makes an exotic finale to a special dinner.

A significant amount of madeira is not made from these grapes, but the more widely planted Tinta Negra Mole variety. These are bottled either as basic madeira (labelled "dry", "medium-dry", "sweet" or, somewhat misleadingly, "finest") or under English-sounding names such as "Duke of Clarence".

Madeira's age is timed from the completion of the *estufagem* (the heating process). The basic styles are released after three years, reserves after five years, special reserves after ten, and vintage wines only after twenty years in cask and two further years in bottle, though they will easily last another twenty to forty years (a fact reflected in their rarity and price). There are also "solera madeiras", which carry the date when the ageing process was first established, such as "Solera 1900". (These shouldn't be confused with vintage madeiras, which are made only from grapes harvested in that year.)

AUSTRALIAN LIQUEUR MUSCAT

Aptly called a "sticky", this highly individual style of dark, sweet, syrupy Muscat with its sumptuously rich, treacle-toffee flavour is a speciality of the Rutherglen region in Victoria. ☆☆

BANYULS, MAURY, AND RIVESALTES

A trio of fortified wines from the Roussillon region in southern France made predominantly from Grenache. When young they tend to be rich, raisiny, and porty. Older versions are often made in what is called a *rancio* style. This indicates a high degree of oxidation giving the wine a sharper, slightly nuttier character that is rather more of an acquired taste. ☆☆

MALAGA

Although málaga, like sherry, encompasses a range of styles, it is most often associated with the intensely sweet, dark, raisiny wine called **Dulce**. Made in Andalucia in southern Spain, it is produced mainly from Pedro Ximénez (the same grape variety that makes the sweetest type of sherry) together with a little Moscatel. It is not strictly a fortified wine but made by a curious amalgam of techniques: part fortified, partly from dried grapes that are fermented, and partly from a boiled dark, treacly concentrate of grape juice. It must be aged in oak for at least two years before release which is carried out in a *solera*-type system (*see* pages 98–9). ☆→☆☆

MARSALA

A Sicilian fortified wine better known for its role in cooking than as a dessert or apéritif wine. As with MALAGA there is a range of styles, though it is the darker, sweeter versions that one encounters most often. The wine is produced from local Grillo and Catarrato grapes fortified to at least seventeen degrees (supplemented by concentrated grape juice) and aged for upwards of a year in oak casks. The basic quality is called "fine" while "superiore" must have an alcohol content of eighteen degrees and have been aged for at least two years (four in the case of a *superiore riserva*). Wines are also labelled by colour – *ambra* (amber), *oro* (gold) and *rubino* (ruby), and by the degree of sweetness – *secco* (dry), *semisecco* (medium-dry), and *dolce* (sweet). The most highly regarded marsala however is **Vergine**, a fine, dry, elegantly nutty wine which has to be aged for at least five years. ☆☆

RASTEAU

The name both of a village in the Côtes du Rhône region and of a rich, spicy, plummy, fortified wine very similar in style to those from Roussillon – BANYULS, MAURY, and RIVESALTES. ☆☆

SETUBAL

Fuller-bodied, often dark, treacly Moscatels such as Setúbal are popular for local consumption throughout Spain and Portugal (*see* also MALAGA), though not much gets exported. ☆→☆☆

Storing and serving

Served in similar ways to other fortified wines – drier wines as apéritifs and sweeter ones at the end of the meal. Madeira has the rare distinction of keeping almost indefinitely once the bottle is open. Also useful to have to hand in the kitchen, as is Marsala which is traditionally used for making zabaglione.

WINE AND FOOD

Just as wine has evolved, so has food. The fairly narrow spectrum of dishes we enjoyed in the past has blossomed into a heady cornucopia of ingredients and flavours. Although in parts of France and Italy people still eat the same kind of food as their parents did, in countries with a less strong cooking tradition, such as the UK, Australia, or the USA, we now borrow ideas and techniques from every corner of the globe.

The effect of this revolution is that a lot of traditional so-called rules about matching food and wine have become irrelevant. At one time the idea that you shouldn't drink red wine with fish made sense. Plainly cooked white fish didn't (and doesn't) go with an astringent tannic red. But season the fish with a spicy marinade, barbecue it, and serve it with a soft fruity New World Pinot Noir and it's sensational.

The truth is that it's misleading to make hard and fast rules. Even if you say that a particular dish normally goes with a particular style of wine, you should really consider how that dish is cooked, whether the wine is typical of its kind and, most importantly, whether you actually like that combination of flavours.

This isn't to argue that it's not worth trying to find a wine that will go reasonably well with what you're eating, more to say that you shouldn't worry too much about finding the perfect match. There are few really dire combinations and a quick check through the following points should help you avoid most of them.

Order of serving The white before red rule may no longer be appropriate, but in most meals it still makes sense to serve drier wines before sweeter ones, younger wines before older vintages, and more light-bodied wines before more full-bodied ones.

Intensity of flavour More useful than the "red wine with meat, white wine with fish" rule is to think about the weight and intensity of flavour of the dish you're serving or ordering. A full-flavoured dish calls for a full-bodied wine (which may well be red), a lighter dish needs a lighter wine. That may come down primarily to the cooking method (or absence of it). Raw, steamed or poached food tends to call for lighter wines, roast and chargrilled dishes for more robust ones.

Which flavours are dominant? Frequently the seasoning which is used in a dish or the sauce in which it is cooked has more effect on the final flavour than the main ingredient. It is more helpful to concentrate on what wines go with, say a Mediterranean style tomato and garlic flavoured sauce or a Thai style stir-fry than to ask yourself which wines go with chicken or pork.

Complement or contrast? You can go for two effects when you choose a wine. Either you can complement the texture and flavour of the dish you're making or you can look for a contrast.

For example, if you were serving a chicken dish with a rich, creamy mushroom sauce you could either go for a smooth, dry white like a Chardonnay with a similarly creamy texture or for an aromatic white like a Riesling which would provide a more exotic note.

If you're unsure what to do just think of it in cooking terms. A crisp, citrussy white will have the same effect on a piece of grilled or fried fish as a squeeze of lemon. If it's a meat dish that requires some sweetness, then serve it with a fruity New World red. If you want to cut the rich, slightly fatty taste of cold roast pork then try a crisp appley white such as dry Chenin Blanc, or a fresh juicy Beaujolais.

Food-friendly wines If you're eating out in a restaurant, you'll often have to choose a bottle that will suit what several people have ordered. And even if you're eating at home, a selection of dishes could be on the table at the same time. What you need is a wine that will go with the maximum number of flavours and offend the least number of people.

My choices would be a lightly oaked or unoaked Chardonnay, a crisp Sauvignon, a New World Pinot Noir or Merlot or a crisp dry rosé. In a restaurant I didn't know, those would tend to be from the New World.

Tried and tested combinations Although it is fun to experiment, do not overlook the conventional options entirely – particularly when it comes to French and Italian food. Most stand the test of time. In a restaurant in a wine-producing area I would always go for the local wine. It will be better value and more likely to suit the style of cooking.

Finally, a word or two to explain the rest of this section. Over the page you'll find suggestions of wines to go with particular styles of cooking and following that there are suggestions of dishes to pair with different styles of wine. The general recommendation in each section applies to most of the individual wines mentioned. The specific suggestions apply more to those wines than the others in that category.

Above *Tangy salad dressings can pose problems for wines and are best accompanied by crisp, fruity whites.*

Far left *The spicy marinades and chargrilled flavours of barbecued food work best with full-flavoured fruity reds and rosés.*

CLASSIC FRENCH

Drinking wine is a way of life in France, so it's no surprise that the food of each major wine region blends seamlessly with its wines. The spiciness of an Alsace Pinot Gris lifts the rich creaminess of a chicken in mushroom sauce; the crisp, acidity of a Muscadet is the ideal partner for the shellfish of the Loire region; the rich casseroles and braises of Burgundian cuisine not only benefit from being cooked in the local wine, but taste good with it too. It makes perfect sense to follow the example of the French and drink the wine of the region.

MEDITERRANEAN

Although mainly associated with the south of France, the Mediterranean style of cooking extends right through southern Europe, encompassing the cooking of Spain, Portugal, and southern Italy. Common to them all are the vivid flavours of tomatoes, peppers, garlic, and olives, together with pungent herbs like basil, rosemary, and oregano. Fish is more common than meat and frequently incorporated into robustly flavoured soups or stews like *bouillabaisse*. Dry, crisp white or rosé (*rosado*) wines often work better than red with this style of food, though light fruity reds are ideal with pizza or *pissaladière*.

NORTHERN ITALY

What is thought of as Italian cooking is fundamentally the cooking of the north and centre of Italy, rather than the south. Nevertheless, even within these boundaries there are major differences between the seafood-based cooking of Venice, for example, and the heartier, more robust cooking of Piedmont. As in France, the local wines are often the best choice. Comparatively neutral, crisp Italian white wines work well with many Italian dishes such as seafood, creamy pasta, classic *risotto*, and *osso buco*. And the marked acidity of many Italian reds is a good foil to richer pasta dishes such as lasagne.

TRADITIONAL BRITISH & IRISH

The British have always had a taste for well-aged wine and, indeed, the plainly cooked roasts, pies, and casseroles that are typical of traditional British and Irish cooking are highly complimentary to delicately flavoured fine wines like mature Rioja, claret, and burgundy. Scotch and Irish salmon is as good as anywhere in the world: simply cooked it is the perfect foil for fine white burgundy, while smoked salmon is surprisingly successful with a wide range of wines including Champagne, Sauvignon Blanc, and manzanilla sherry. Traditional English cheeses can be among the easiest to pair with fine wines. Port and stilton is a classic combination but you could try the attractive *vin doux naturels* from the south of France like Banyuls or Rivesaltes.

CENTRAL & EASTERN EUROPEAN

Again the cooking of central Europe such as Germany, Austria, and Hungary is relatively plain, but often involves some tricky matches for wine such as smoked meats and *sauerkraut*. Crisp, dry whites are generally a better solution than reds. Riesling is perfect with the local cuisine, especially pork or fish dishes with a creamy sauce. Austria and Hungary, with their love of paprika, have a slightly more robust style of cooking. Crisp, dry whites will cope, as will peppery reds like Austria's Blaufränkisch. And again, dry whites, especially Chasselas, are the answer for the many cooked cheese dishes of Switzerland.

SCANDINAVIAN

With its emphasis on pickled foods, Scandinavia is more beer and schnapps than natural wine territory. But dry Gemanic style whites work better than anything else. The famous Swedish dish *gravadlax* (cured salmon with a dill and mustard sauce) is easier to pair with wine than it sounds, and goes well with either a German Riesling or Demi-Sec Vouvray. Here there is also a fondness for serving meat with tart red fruit, like cranberries and lingonberries. This works well with a soft, fruity red like a Cabernet/Merlot.

MIDDLE EASTERN/NORTH AFRICAN

The southern half of the Mediterranean – Greece, Turkey, and the Lebanon – has a more robust palate of flavours including lemon, garlic, and raw onion, and spices such as coriander and cumin. The typical style of eating is to put several dishes on the table at once which calls for an all-purpose wine that will cope with a wide range of flavours – a crisp, dry white or dry rosé works best. The grilled meats of the region suit light, fruity reds, while the more spicy *tagines* or couscous of Morocco call for a more vigorous, home-grown Syrah or a Côtes du Rhône-Villages.

INDIAN

The widely held belief that Indian food doesn't go with wine rests on the assumption that it is all searingly hot. In fact, it embraces a wide range of different styles from the mild kormas of the north to the much spicier dishes of the south. The problem is you often get dishes of varying degrees of heat in the same meal. You could replicate the refreshing quality of lager by serving a clean, crisp, dry, neutral white or rosé. Alternatively, try serving a much fruitier New World style of wine such as an unoaked Chardonnay or a jammy Cabernet or Shiraz.

SOUTHEAST ASIAN

Also hot, but less spicy than Indian food, its distinguishing flavours – lemongrass, galangal, and fresh coriander are quite wine friendly. Try crisp citrussy whites like Sauvignon Blanc or more neutral Austrian Grüner Veltliner. Alsace Pinot Gris also works well, as does Semillon and Australian Riesling.

CHINESE

As with India, people often think of Chinese food as just one style, but there are marked differences between the delicate, subtlety of Cantonese cuisine and the more fiery flavours of Szechuan cooking. The conventional match with the former are aromatic whites such as Riesling and Gewürztraminer, although Viognier would also work and a Blanc de Blancs Champagne can be sensational with lighter dishes. With more robust dishes switch to a light, fruity red like a Beaujolais cru or Merlot, or a fruity rosé.

JAPANESE

One of the trickier cuisines to pair with wine – the Japanese traditionally drink saké. With raw fish dishes like *sushi* and *sashimi* you want an ultra-dry white like Muscadet, Chablis or even an extra-brut Champagne. With more spicy, savoury *teppanyaki* dishes or a *teriyaki* sauce, a fruity, but not too oaky red like a Chilean Merlot or Carmenère would be a better choice. (N.B. Hot and sour Japanese pickles are particularly tough on wine – try to avoid them if you're drinking anything decent.)

PACIFIC RIM

This style of cooking – developed in Australia, New Zealand, and along the West Coast of America – is heavily influenced by Southeast Asia. It therefore goes best with similar types of wine to those cuisines – vivid New World Sauvignons, Rieslings, and other aromatic wines like Pinot Gris and Grüner Veltliner. The use of chargrilling can add a smoky note which is best offset by a fruity red like a Pinot Noir or a lighter Shiraz or Merlot.

CAJUN, CENTRAL & SOUTH AMERICAN

This characterful style of cooking is dominated by spicy chillies and big, gutsy flavours that need correspondingly powerful wines to complement them. These are the perfect dishes to show off lush, full-bodied reds like California Zinfandel, Chilean Cabernets or Merlots or Argentinian Syrah or Malbec. For whites, look to zesty Chilean or South African Sauvignon Blancs (a good match for *ceviche* or *guacamole*).

AFRO/CARIBBEAN

With hot, spicy dishes like jerk chicken, curry goat, and pepperpot, this is again a flavourful style of cooking that needs correspondingly full-flavoured wines such as a tropical fruity Chardonnay or a rich, plummy Shiraz.

MIX AND MATCH MENUS

This is the kind of contemporary cuisine you'll find in fashionable restaurants in every capital city of the world. It borrows from every culinary tradition – from Italian to Japanese – and encompasses every type of flavour. The pick and mix nature of the menu can make it difficult to find a bottle to suit every dish: so take advantage of wines that are available by the glass (as many are in these restaurants). Lighter Chardonnays, Sauvignon Blancs, and New World Pinot Noirs all go well with this style of food, but this cuisine is all about breaking rules, so don't be afraid to break wine rules too. Seared tuna, for example, is just as good with a light red wine as a white.

TRADITIONAL AMERICAN

Unlike French or Italian food, traditional American food didn't grow up side by side with wine and many Americans, particularly in the deep south, still wouldn't drink it at all. Homely dishes like fried chicken and meatloaf taste best with simple, light reds or smooth, creamy whites. A classic American barbecue with sweet, sticky ribs needs something a bit fuller-bodied – ideally an all-American Zinfandel. For a creamy fish chowder try a lightly oaked or unoaked Chardonnay.

CRISP, FRESH, DRY WHITES

General Summery food – salads and steamed, grilled or barbecued fish. Mediterranean fish soups and stews. Fish and chips. Light stir-fries, noodle dishes, mild curries.

Chablis (unoaked) Oysters, seafood, shellfish.

Muscadet *Moules marinières, plateau de fruits de mer*, oysters, sushi.

Sauvignon Blanc Seafood and shellfish. Asparagus. Grilled vegetables. Sancerre and other Loire Sauvignons: particularly good with goat's cheese. New World Sauvignon: dishes flavoured with garlic, ginger, and coriander.

Pinot Grigio, Soave, and other Italian whites *Antipasti*. Light pastas with a seafood or light tomato sauce (*e.g. linguine* with clams) or creamy sauces (*spaghetti carbonara*) or with pesto. *Gnocchi, risotto*, seafood salad, chargrilled squid, *fritto misto*.

Grüner Veltliner and young, dry Riesling Light, south-east Asian-influenced dishes.

SMOOTH, MEDIUM-BODIED WHITES

General Salmon. Fish, chicken, pork or veal with creamy sauces. Roast or grilled chicken. Chicken pie. Escalopes of chicken or veal. Egg-based dishes such as omelettes, quiches or souffles. Creamy pasta dishes.

Alsace Pinot Blanc *Quiche Lorraine*.

Burgundy Plainly cooked (*e.g.* poached) salmon, Dover sole, turbot. Langoustines. Roast turkey.

Chardonnay and Chardonnay blends Lighter more citrussy styles: cooked fish dishes such as fish cakes, fish pies, seared scallops. Sweeter, fruitier styles such as **Semillon/Chardonnay**: spicy chicken and pork dishes.

Chenin Blanc *See* lighter styles of Chardonnay.

Colombard *See* Semillon-Chardonnay.

RICH, FULL-BODIED WHITES

General Classic *haute cuisine*. Richly flavoured chicken, fish, and shellfish. Buttery sauces.

Chardonnay European style (burgundian, Californian): rich lobster and shellfish dishes, fine white fish such as halibut and turbot.
New World style (Australian): robustly flavoured or spiced chicken, pork and fish dishes. Steak if you enjoy a white wine with it.

Pessac-Léognan/Graves *See* European style Chardonnay.

Semillon Full-flavoured chicken and pork dishes. Southeast Asian/Pacific Rim cuisine.

Viognier *See* New World Chardonnay.

AROMATIC & MEDIUM-DRY WHITES

General Hard to generalize because this category encompasses so many contrasting styles. Most aromatic wines have some affinity with creamy sauces and with slightly spicy food.

Gewürztraminer Chinese meat dishes especially duck. Thai and milder Indian curries. Pungent cheeses (especially Munster).

Riesling German Kabinett: light fish and meat dishes. Salmon and trout (particularly with a creamy sauce). Smoked meats, salads, lightly seasoned stir-fries. *Choucroute*. Spätlese: duck, and goose. Alsace: similar to German Riesling but can take slightly richer flavours. Australian: excellent with Thai and other Southeast Asian food.

Tokay-Pinot Gris Rich poultry and pork dishes. Thai food.

Vouvray and other medium-dry whites Chicken or pork dishes with creamy, slightly sweet sauces or in dishes which incorporate fruit, like apricots and peaches.

LIGHT, FRUITY REDS

General A wide range of cold and cured meats, simply grilled chicken, pork, and veal. Robustly seasoned and barbecued fish dishes. Mediterranean-style food, stuffed vegetables.

Beaujolais-Villages *Charcuterie*. Cold roast ham (and boiled or grilled gammon). Creamy, soft rind cheeses like Brie and Camembert.

Côtes du Rhône Sausage and mash.

Chinon and other Loire reds Seared salmon and tuna. Also good with goat's cheese

Pinot Noir Burgundy (lighter styles): charcuterie, simply roast or grilled game. New World: seared and chargrilled meat and fish.

Tempranillo Robust Spanish-style chicken and pork dishes flavoured with *pimenton*.

Valpolicella and other Italian reds Most types of pasta (except those with creamy and seafood sauces). Pizza, Italian-style sausages.

SMOOTH, MEDIUM-BODIED REDS

General Most types of meat, especially plainly cooked beef and lamb and homely dishes like shepherds pie and sausages.

Beaujolais Cru Duck, rabbit, roast or braised veal.

Bordeaux Roast beef and lamb, lighter stews and casseroles, and hard cheeses.

Burgundy Roast game, venison, kidneys, *coq au vin, boeuf bourguignon*, dishes containing mushrooms, soft rind cheeses.

Chianti and other Italian reds Grilled and roast pork and lamb, steak, calves liver, richer pasta dishes like *cannelloni* and lasagne.

Merlot (New World style) Chargrilled meat and vegetables.

Rioja and Navarra Grilled lamb, particularly with herbs. Hard cheeses.

FULL-BODIED REDS

General Chargrilled steaks, casseroles, spicy meat, and vegetarian dishes such as *goulash*.

Barbaresco and Barolo Rich meat and game, especially hare. Mushrooms and truffles.

Cabernet Sauvignon Cheaper bottles: medium hot curries, chilli con carne, and other spicy meat dishes. Serious bottles: more classic red meat dishes, but can take robust seasoning.

Fitou and other southern French reds Cassoulet, duck confit, lamb with flageolets.

Hermitage (Rhône reds) Big braises and *daubes*.

Shiraz *See* Cabernet Sauvignon.

Zinfandel Oxtail, chilli dishes, barbecued ribs.

AGED REDS & RARITIES

Aged reds Older versions of classic wines like Bordeaux, burgundy, and Rioja will go with similar types of dishes to more recent vintages, but keep the food simple. Older wines go particularly well with game.

Rarities Take a similar approach to older wines. Keep the food simple.

Amarone Richly sauced meat and game. Cheese.

Salice Salentino and other southern Italian reds Robustly cooked meat and vegetable dishes (especially aubergine), hard cheeses.

ROSES

General Similar dishes to crisp, dry whites. Milder curries and other lightly spiced dishes.

Provençal and Rhône rosés Typically Mediterranean dishes such as *aioli*, *salade niçoise*, *bouillabaisse*, and *ratatouille*.

Bordeaux rosé Elegant summery fish and chicken.

New World rosé Pacific Rim cuisine, barbecues.

Rosado (Spanish rosé) *Paella*, couscous, *tapas*.

Rosé d'Anjou and other medium-dry rosés Chicken or prawn salads.

CHAMPAGNE & SPARKLING WINES

General Lighter styles: go with similar food to crisp, dry whites. Fuller styles: with the same type of food as good quality white burgundy.

Lighter styles (NV, Blanc de Blancs) *Canapés*, caviar, smoked salmon, *sushi*, shellfish, scrambled eggs, Chinese (Cantonese) food.

Richer, toastier styles (vintage, prestige cuvées, quality New World sparkling wines) Richly sauced seafood and shellfish. Lightly sauced chicken and pork dishes.

Demi-Sec Lightly spiced dishes. Creamy sauces.

Sweet Light fruit-based desserts. Fruit salad, mousses, meringues, and creamy gâteaux go well with sweet Italian sparklers such as Asti.

Rose Lightly spiced Chinese and Southeast Asian food. Richer wines can be drunk with rare lamb, pork, and plainly cooked game birds.

Red Barbecues and Christmas turkey.

SWEET WINES

General Fruit-based and creamy puddings are the easiest to match, chocolate the trickiest. The wine should be sweeter than the pudding. Try lighter sweet wines with creamy blue cheeses.

Australian Liqueur Muscat Pecan pie, walnut tart, mince pies, coffee cake, vanilla ice cream.

Beerenauslese and other German and Austrian sweet wines Simple fruit tarts.

Late Harvest Riesling and Semillon (New World) Exotic fruit salads, Southeast Asian influenced desserts.

Mavrodaphne of Patras and other sweet red wines Dark chocolate cake and puddings.

Muscat de Beaumes-de-Venise and other southern French Muscats Strawberries and cream, fruit tarts, crumbles, Christmas pudding.

Moscatel de Valencia Citrus based desserts *e.g.* oranges in caramel, *crêpes suzette*, trifle.

Orange Muscat Fruit salads, orange flavoured puddings, white or milk chocolate, desserts.

Sauternes and other sweet Bordeaux Fruit tarts, *crème brûlée*, fois gras. Roquefort.

Tokaj *Tarte tatin*, bread and butter pudding, Stilton.

Vendange Tardive (Alsace) *Foie gras*, fruit tarts.

Vouvray and other sweet Loire wines Pear and apple tarts or flans.

FORTIFIED WINES

Amontillado and dry oloroso sherry; bual and verdelho madeira An alternative to port with cheese. Nut tarts. Turron.

Banyuls, Rivesaltes, and other *vins doux naturels* Chocolate desserts, desserts with prunes. Blue cheese.

Fino and manzanilla sherry; sercial madeira; white port As an apéritif with olives and nuts, *chorizo* sausage, *tortilla*, and other *tapas*.

Marsala *Zabaglione* (to make), almond cake.

Ruby port styles (Late Bottled Vintage, vintage character) Chocolate cake. Blue cheese.

Sweet oloroso sherry; malmsey madeira Baked apples. Christmas cake and pudding, vanilla ice cream.

Tawny port styles Hard cheeses. Walnut tart and other nut-and-caramel based desserts.

Vintage port Stilton and other traditional British and Irish cheeses.

STORAGE, SERVING, AND WINE FAULTS

Few people believe that they have anything to do with the way a wine tastes. They imagine that once the wine is bottled it continues to taste the same way until you open it. But the way you store and serve a wine has a marked effect on the way it ends up in the glass.

Storing wine

Unless you drink a bottle of wine within a month or two of bringing it home, it may start to change its character. Whether or not that's a good thing depends on the type of wine and your own taste. An inexpensive young, crisp white loses its freshness quite rapidly and certainly won't improve from being kept for more than a few months. A full-bodied red, on the other hand, may well benefit from being laid down in a cool dark place for a year or so, which will enable more complex mellow flavours to develop.

The problem is that you don't always know how old a wine is when you buy it. At one extreme it may be just a few weeks old. Wineries these days are under considerable pressure to release their wines as quickly as possible. The sooner they do, the sooner they get paid, so the wine can still be in a state of "bottle shock" and may actually improve from being allowed to lie down quietly for a few weeks. For this reason it is best to avoid a wine that a shop proudly announces has just arrived, unless you are prepared to give it a rest.

At the other extreme are wines that may have been hanging around on a shelf or in a restaurant cellar for months. Hot bright lights can be particularly damaging, so it's best to avoid a bottle that has been sitting under a spotlight, particularly if it feels warm to the touch. Shops will often sell off stock that is near the end of its shelf-life as a "bin end" – which can be a good deal provided you drink it straight away. As a rule of thumb, if the date strikes you as old, don't attempt to store it for any length of time.

Most inexpensive and medium-priced wines are designed to be drunk more or less immediately, so it's not worth buying more than you're likely to need for the next couple of months. Storage becomes more of an issue with better quality white and red wines, particularly those from Bordeaux and Burgundy, that are only affordable if you buy them when they're first released.

With reds the temptation is always to keep them for too long, the theory being that if they're older they must be better. In my experience, however, it's far more common to be disappointed by a bottle that's been kept for too long, than one that's been opened too soon. Only a small handful of very expensive wines, like top German Rieslings, sweet Loire whites, and big, full-bodied Rhône reds that can be impossibly tough and tannic in their youth, repay cellaring for a decade or more.

Storage options

Unfortunately, few of us have houses with cellars, but that doesn't mean there aren't other places which are perfectly good for storing wine. What's good about a cellar is that it is cool, dark, and damp, so wine remains at a constant temperature and corks don't dry out.

What wine doesn't like is warmth, vibration, and wildly fluctuating temperatures. Unsuitable places include areas like uninsulated garages or outside buildings which get very hot in summer and cold in winter (lighter wines will freeze if the temperature actually drops much below freezing) or, as many people do in fact store it, in a bright warm kitchen on top of a fridge or next to a boiler.

If you have no more than a couple of cases, the best place to put them is in a cupboard in a spare bedroom, or under the stairs at a temperature that doesn't exceed 20°C (68°F) or drop below 10°C (50°F). You need to take care that it's free from extraneous smells such as chemicals, paint or cleaning products, and that the bottles are stored on their side so that the wine is in touch with the cork and air can't seep into the bottle. You also need a reasonable degree of humidity (this can be achieved simply by putting a bowl of water on the floor).

If you are serious about collecting wine, you can buy temperature-controlled cabinets or even have a purpose-built spiral cellar installed, but unless you are nursing a particularly valuable collection, it is a substantial investment to make. It may, in fact, be more practical to get the company you buy the wine from to store it for you, though you should only do this if you are dealing with a reputable and well-established dealer. While it does mean your wine is likely to be stored in near-perfect conditions, it does of course have the drawback that you can't pull out a bottle when the mood takes you.

Serving

There's still a mystique surrounding the serving of wine which is actually a great deal less complicated than it sometimes sounds. Nevertheless, it is true that you can actually make wine taste better if you give a little bit of care and attention to the way you serve it.

Above *A temperature-controlled cabinet such as this – just like a fridge but specially designed for wine – is ideal for homes with limited cellaring facilities.*

Far left *A traditional underground cellar, for those fortunate enough to have one, is the ideal choice for long-term personal wine storage.*

Temperature

The thing that will make the biggest difference to your enjoyment of a glass of wine is the temperature at which you serve it. The conventional wisdom is that whites should be served chilled and reds at room temperature. But that begs the question of how cold your fridge is or how warm a room you leave it in. These days, with rooms regularly heated to at least 20°C (68°F), there's a danger that if you leave a red wine out too long it will get unpleasantly soupy. Most reds, in fact, are better for being left in a relatively cool place before serving, with light, fruity reds, even benefiting from half an hour in the fridge.

With whites there tends to be the opposite danger of chilling them too much, which can dull their aroma and flavour. While light, crisp whites, aromatic whites, and sweet and sparkling wines benefit from being quite cold (at least an hour in the average fridge), richer, fuller-bodied whites can be served a little warmer (chill them for about forty-five minutes). If you are served a glass of wine that is too cold you can warm it up by cupping your hands round the glass.

Changing the temperature quickly

If you are caught unprepared you can chill a wine quickly by plunging the bottle into a bucket of iced water (quicker than just ice) or by popping it in the freezer for twenty minutes (though don't whatever you do forget that you've put it there). You can now also buy insulated "jackets" which you keep in the freezer and slip over the bottle as needed. If you need to warm up a wine slightly (for instance, a full-bodied red that has been kept in an unheated room) place the bottle in a bowl or bucket of warm water.

Pulling the cork

There's a general idea that you need to open a bottle of red wine at least an hour in advance of drinking it. In fact, the act of pulling the cork – or unscewing the cap – doesn't benefit the wine hugely if you don't pour anything out of the bottle. The point about opening a wine in advance (other than to check it's not corked) is to get air into it in order to open up the flavours. Traditionally, that used to be done with reds that were likely to be tough or tannic, but the majority of wines these days don't really need opening up in this way. If you do have a wine that you think can benefit from aerating – and that can include full-bodied whites as well as particularly robust full-bodied reds – you might just as well decant it.

Decanting

The whole idea of decanting makes people nervous. In fact, it's nothing more than pouring wine from one container to another, exposing it to the air and helping to release its aromas. To do this, simply transfer it straight into a clean jug or decanter. If you don't want to have a jug on the table just pour the wine carefully back into the bottle again. This is referred to as double-decanting.

The other reason to decant is because the wine has accumulated a heavy deposit or sediment that you don't want to end up in your glass. If you're dealing with this kind of wine (or port) leave the bottle upright for at least twenty-four hours (preferably for a couple of days), then, with a light placed behind the bottle (a lamp or a torch will do), steadily pour the wine, stopping when the sediment reaches the neck of the bottle. It is not difficult, simply a matter of having a watchful eye and a steady hand. Again you can return the wine to the original bottle having rinsed it well first.

There are wines that do not benefit from decanting, particularly fine old red wines whose fragile aromas and complex flavours can rapidly evaporate once exposed to the air. Another wine, ironically, is dry sherry which rapidly loses its fresh, tangy character if stored, as frequently used to be the case, in a decanter.

Glasses

People tend to choose glasses more for their looks than for their suitability for drinking wine, but the shape and thickness of a glass can have a marked effect on flavour. The problem with the basic "Paris goblet" type of wine glass is that it's too small and delivers the wine in a rush, so that you've barely tasted it before swallowing it.

What you need is a plain, clear glass with a generously sized bowl that tapers slightly towards the rim so you can swirl the wine around to release and enjoy its aromas. The stem of the glass should be long enough so that you don't have to hold it by the bowl (otherwise the heat of your hand will warm the wine) and it should have a fine thin rim which makes it easier to sip and savour the wine rather than just gulp it down. As a counsel of perfection, you would have a different type of glass for each style of wine. In fact, there is an Austrian glass designer, Georg Riedel, who has produced just that and there's no doubt that the right shaped glass enhances the varietal character and style of a particular wine. But given that not many of us can afford a wardrobe of different

Above *The intriguing sight of a wine glass being blown. The quality and shape of wine glasses can have a surprising influence on the appreciation of a wine's aromas and flavours.*

Far left *Decanting a wine is not only desirable to remove any sediment that might have accumulated but can also open up the flavour.*

glasses, a more realistic target would be a largeish wine glass of the type I've described above for full-bodied white and most red wines, a slightly smaller wine glass for more aromatic white wines and light reds, a small "copita" type sherry glass which would also double for port and dessert wines, and a tall Champagne "flute". If you can only afford one of these extras I would go for the flute. It traps the Champagne bubbles and aromas far more effectively than a saucer-shaped glass.

Keeping glasses clean

It is also important that your glasses, whatever their shape, should be scrupulously clean. Grease, dust, and detergent residues can all affect the taste of your wine. The most efficient way to wash your glasses is to run them through a dishwasher without any detergent, though repeated use can scratch fine glasses. Personally, I think it's better to wash them as soon as possible in the hottest water you can bear, rinse them, and dry them immediately with a clean linen tea towel. Either way you should store them upright rather than upended or you'll trap any stale air.

Pouring

When you're pouring wine you should only fill the glass half to two-thirds full. The problem is that this may be misinterpreted as lack of generosity, but if you want to enjoy a wine's aromas, which are half the pleasure of tasting, you need to leave room to swirl it around.

Order of serving

Without being unnecessarily hidebound about it, it does make sense to follow the conventional serving order for most wines. In just the way that you wouldn't serve a robust casserole before a light fish dish, or a pudding before your main course, so it makes sense to serve a light wine before a powerfully concentrated one and a dry wine before a sweet one. There is, however, no reason why you shouldn't serve a light red before a rich, full-bodied white: weight is more important than colour.

Leftovers

After the first hour or two, the exposure to air that was so beneficial on first opening the bottle starts reacting adversely on the wine and will eventually turn it to vinegar. So, if you have half a bottle or less left over try and decant it into a smaller bottle, recork it, then pop it into the fridge. (It's well worth keeping one or two half bottles for this purpose.)

There are also wine preservation systems which pump air out of the bottle or ones that pump in a layer of inert gas. Some people swear by them but, to be honest, I don't think they're a great deal better than replacing the cork – maybe because wine is never lying around our house for that long. You can buy special stoppers to keep the fizz in Champagne and other sparkling wines. Dessert wines will stay fresh longer than most table wines, as will most types of port and sherry (except fino and manzanilla which should be treated like white wine). But they should still be drunk in weeks rather than months.

Wine faults

There are certain quirky characteristics of particular types of wine that you can imagine are faults if you haven't come across them before. The coarse sweaty smell of Sauvignon Blanc which is sometimes rudely compared to cat's pee, the odd, slightly petrolly smell of mature Riesling, the rank farmyardy aromas of aged burgundy, although sometimes unappetizing, are within the normal range of aromas and flavours that can be expected from these wines. But if you encounter any of the following aromas (in most cases you don't actually have to taste a wine to tell that it's faulty) you can safely assume something is seriously wrong:

- A musty, mouldy, dank smell. If it's just a faint trace it may be what's called "bottle stink" – a pocket of stale air trapped in the bottle which will clear within about ten to fifteen minutes of opening. If it doesn't or the smell becomes more pronounced it's more likely that the cork is contaminated, *i.e.* that the wine is "corked".
- White wine with slightly brackish, sherried smell, usually combined with a dark yellow colour is likely to be oxidized and therefore well past its best.
- A strong smell of bad eggs or drains. This indicates an excess of sulphur in the wine.
- A thin, very sharp wine. Everyone's tolerance of acid in wine varies, but if it's mouthpuckeringly sour, it shouldn't be.
- A stewed, baked, slightly flabby character in reds usually means the fermentation temperature has been allowed to rise too high and the wine is over-extracted. Not undrinkable, but unpleasant.

Above *Screwcaps have become increasingly acceptable as a wine closure – avoiding the risk of cork taint. The jury is still out on whether it affects the ageing potential of fine wines.*

Far left *The cork oak unlike other trees, allows its thick spongey bark to be stripped off without the rest of the tree being harmed. The quality of the cork is crucial – if it is contaminated, it can cause faulty or "corked" wines which will smell dank or musty. This faulty wine (**right**) should be a pale golden yellow, but, because too much air has got in through the cork (oxidation), it is now an unattractive dull, dark yellow.*

INDEX

Indexer's note: Grape varieties and wines made from the same varieties are indexed together, as are places or vineyards and wines named after them. *Italic pagination* refers to illustration captions.

ACKNOWLEDGMENTS

Particular thanks for this revised edition should go to my original copy editor Lucy Bridgers who painstakingly went through the text and to oenologist Gerd Stepp of Marks and Spencer who checked the viticultural and winemaking sections. Thanks to all at Mitchell Beazley especially my patient editor, Juanne Branquinho and to Hilary Lumsden and Jane Aspen for their enthusiasm about updating and reissuing the book. Finally, a big thank you to my husband, Trevor, who first introduced me to the pleasures of good wine.

t = top; b = bottom; c = centre

Cephas Picture Library/Mick Rock 33, 114. **Claes Löfgren** 28, 49, 72, 87, 37, 43. **Copyright © Octopus Publishing Group Ltd** 104, 105, 112. **Corbis UK Ltd/Morton Beebe** 83. **Patrick Eagar** 16, 17, 19, 79. **Armin Faber** 26, 29. **Getty Images Ltd./The Tony Stone Collection** 86, 100. **Hilary Lumsden** 78. **Krista Kennell/ZUMA/Corbis** 115. **Robert Harding Picture Library** 113t/**Liaison Int.** 110. **Image Bank/Michael Melford** 30. **Brian Jordan** 36. **Reed Consumer Books Limited/James Johnson** 8, 9, 111b/**Ray Moller** 33b/**Steven Morris** 11b, 37b, 39b, 41b, 43b, 45b, 47b, 49b, 51 b, 53 b, 55 b, 57b, 59b, 61b, 63b, 65b, 67b, 69b, 71b, 73b, 75b, 77b, 79b, 81b, 83b, 85b, 87b, 89b, 91b, 93b, 95b, 97b, 99b, 101b, 103 b, 105b, 113 b, 113 c 115 b. **Janet Price** 13, 15, 21, 23, 42, 55. **Root Stock/Tessa van der Haar** 24/**Hendrik Holler** 10, 11, 12, 14, 18, 22, 32, 48, 54, 66, 67, 93, 98. **Scope/Jean- Luc Barde** 60, 111t/ **Bernard Galeron** 61/**Philip Gould** 20/**Jacques Guillard** 73, 82/**Michel Guillard** 25, 27, 92/**Noel Hautemaniere** 102/**Francis Jalain** 31.

Author photography: **Ian Cook**

The author and publishers would also like to thank:
Oddbins Ltd for supplying the wines for photography.
Michael Johnson (Ceramics) Ltd for the loan of Riedel wine glasses.